MY
MEMOIRS

INCLUDING THREE YEARS IN PAX AND HIKING THE APPALACHIAN TRAIL

———————————

Omar Lapp

My Memoirs
Including Three Years in Pax and Hiking the Appalachian Trail

by Omar Lapp

Library of Congress Number: 2017959407
International Standard Book Number: 978-1-60126-558-6

My Memoirs is available for purchase at
MASTHOF BOOKSTORE
219 Mill Road, Morgantown, PA 19543
610-286-0258
orders@masthof.com

𝔐𝔞𝔰𝔱𝔥𝔬𝔣 𝔓𝔯𝔢𝔰𝔰
219 Mill Road | Morgantown, PA 19543-9516
www.Masthof.com

With love to my wife, Sara,
and our four children,
Nathan, Michael, Irene and Herman

Thanks to granddaughter Ellen
for typing the manuscript taken from my handwriting.
Thanks to Sara and Irene for your
editing and proofreading.

Table of Contents

Introduction

If you buy this book it is at your own risk. This book is not guaranteed to be interesting. When I retired from my retirement job at age 87 I needed something to do. What you have in your hand is what I did. If someone gave you this book your only loss is shelf space. I enjoyed reliving much of my life as I wrote these memoirs. Some sections I wrote because I remembered them. But for much of what I wrote I had diaries and journals that helped me to remember, especially names of places and dates. I'm aware many of the details included will not be of interest to everyone but they were important to me so I included them. You can practice speed reading, skimming and skipping which is okay.

If you read some or all of this book and would like to respond by phone or email I'd be glad to hear from you. And let me know a little of what's happening in your life but not too much so I still have time to take a nap if I need one. May the Lord's blessing be on everyone reading this.

Omar Lapp, August 2017
717-442-4465
omarsara@epix.net

CHAPTER 1

A Few Early Memories

My grandfather, John Henry Lapp, died two months after I turned two. Sometime before he died, grandfather was lying on the floor in their living room and I was crawling all over him. I vividly remember how much fun it was and how good I felt. I'm quite sure it's my earliest memory. Grandpa was a deacon in the Lower Pequea District of the Amish Church.

Grandmother, Rachel Stoltzfus Lapp, died when I was four. I remember her sitting on a large chair by the window beside her dining room table and I would talk with her. I faintly remember her smoking a pipe. I'm told that some but not many older Amish women in her generation did smoke. I know her mother, Sarah Mast Stoltzfus, smoked a pipe. Her son David Lapp, my uncle, has that written in his memoir. Grandpa and Grandma lived in the "Dauty End" (Grandparent End) of our house. The house was built by my great grandparents David and Sara Mast Stoltzfus in 1879, just east of Route 897 on present Buena Vista Road.

When I was two or three I remember an event when our church service was at Jake's Bens. After the worship service and after lunch, (I remember neither) I was with Mother and the women. Mother asked me to go tell Dad she is ready to go home. I went to the room where the men were standing and visiting. I walked by their many black pant legs which I clearly remember. I grabbed Dad's pant leg, looked up and said, "Da Mam iss ready fa hame

gehe." (Mother is ready to go home) But it wasn't Dad!! It was Steff.
I was very embarrassed.

A related memory when I was probably four. I was in our
yard near the road when I saw Dad coming by on his one-horse
spring wagon. I ran to the road and said, "Dat, Ich vill aue mitt
gehe." (Dad, I want to go along too) But it wasn't Dad!! It was Steff.
Another embarrassment.

Fast forward eight years. My sister Lena had just married
Benjamin B. Beiler. Dad accompanied them to visit an attorney in
Lancaster. Dad was signing a paper when he noticed someone else
in the room. Dad got up and said, "Vell Steff, bischt du awe doh?"
(Well Steve, are you here also). To Dad's embarrassment, no one
was there, just a mirror.

A scene I can still visualize I saw probably at age three. My
sister Lizzie had accompanied me to the lookout on top of the fourteen story Griest Building at Penn Square in Lancaster. I peered
down and there were toy cars, trucks and trolleys coming west on
King Street and going north on Queen. The toy vehicles fascinated
me! The disappointment was when we came down. I asked Lizzie
where the toy cars were that I had seen. She tried to explain to me
that from a distance objects appear smaller. This was difficult for
me to comprehend.

Sometime before 1935 Dad bought a second farm a mile
east of the farm on which he was born and fixed it up to be able
to milk twenty-four holstein cows. He frequently had Lancaster
County Farm Bureau Agent Dutch Bucher give advice on how to
make the farm more productive. Mr. Bucher usually came in a motorcycle with a sidecar attached. On one occasion Dad went with
Mr. Bucher to the recently purchased farm in the sidecar and I sat
on Dad's lap. I have a rather clear memory of traveling the straight
stretch of road just east of our farm in the sidecar sitting on Dad's
lap. I was four years old and in my glory.

Soon after I was five we moved from Clear View Farm just east of Route 897 to Lone Star Farm along what is now Old Mill Road where I grew up. A memory from there when I was five before starting school is sitting on the floor on our dining/living room facing Mother. Mother was on her rocking chair teaching me a bedtime prayer. I memorized the prayer and knelt by my bed every night and repeated it before retiring for many years.

This is the prayer:

Müde bin Ich, gehe zu ruh
Schliese meine müde Augen zu
Ich bin noch schwach, Ich bin noch klein
Du grosser Gott wollst bei mir sein Amen

Translated:

I'm tired, I'm going to rest
I'm closing my tired eyes
I am still weak, I am still small
You great God will be with me Amen

I will mention this prayer again in chapter 12.

Because almost no cars were on the roads near Lone Star Farm, Dad occasionally sent me with our one-horse spring wagon on a short errand when I was only seven or eight years old. On one such occasion my younger brother John was with me. And as we came onto what is now Buena Vista Road we did meet a car with two men in it. They stopped to talk to these two little Amish boys. Among other things they asked if we knew where Willis Weaver lived. I said I did not know of a Willis Weaver. I did tell them, however, that a Villis Vayva lived on the farm across the meadow. They laughed and thanked me. I informed Dad about it and asked why they laughed. He said that Willis Weaver was the same as Villis Vayva. I found that information very interesting.

My sister Lizzie married in 1936 to Harvey E. Miller from Indiana and moved to Indiana. Lizzie and Harvey met in Florida. In July 1937 Dad hired Frank Martin from north of Blue Ball to take our family, Lena, John, Mother, Dad and me to visit Harvey and Lizzie whose home was four miles west of Nappanee, Indiana. I think Frank had a 1935 Model A Ford Sedan. His top speed was 45 mph. It took us three days to drive the 620 miles. We took Route 30 to Indiana and at Ft. Wayne, Indiana we went north to Route 6. Nappanee is on Route 6. We slept in cabins two nights on the way. Cabins were before motels as a place to sleep. Following are several things that impressed me in Indiana: The Amish all had bicycles and used them a lot. The men and boys wore store bought straw hats rather than homemade. Their buggies had solid rubber on the wheel rims rather than steel. These are memories of mine when I was seven.

A highlight of my growing up years was our trip to Indiana every other year. In 1939 my brother Seth took us in his, I think, 1937 Oldsmobile. It only took us two days. In 1941 Dad's brother David took us. During the war years, 1943 and 1945, we went by train and saw lots of soldiers on the train. Some years later Dad took each of his Pennsylvania grandchildren as pre-teens to visit their cousins in Indiana, usually three or four at a time. I think visiting Indiana as a boy helped me feel good about being Amish.

The last memory I'll share is not really something I remember but my sister Lena told me. Some weeks after I was born Mother would tell Lena to pull out the lower drawer of the dry sink, fix a blanket in it and put Omar in it which Lena says she did many times. The dry sink with the drawer is still in our family. Our daughter Irene in Colorado has it and uses it. I would like to see that drawer again sometime.

CHAPTER 2

Elementary School Days

My Dad, Mose Lapp, was forty-five years older than I. However we both went to the same one-room school in Buena Vista. Dad walked a half mile from the west and years later I walked a half mile from the east. Dad and I also had the same teacher. Miss Leila Oberholser was the teacher of Buena Vista School for the 1892-1893 school years when Dad was probably in second grade. She was also teacher 1914-1917 and again in 1935-1936 when I was in first grade. Dad enjoyed school and went until he was sixteen. He only went through the winter months however. I somewhat enjoyed school but usually did not admit it as boys were not expected to say they liked school.

Buena Vista was a public school from 1867-1962. It is now an Amish school. My school years were 1935 to 1943. Five of us were in first grade together, Reuben Lantz, David Allgyer, Lizzie Beiler, Lydia Stoltzfus and I. David's family moved to Upper Mill Creek after his first year and I did not stay in close touch. Reuben was my best friend all my school years. Eighty-two years later as I write this all five of us are still living. Reuben has lived his adult years in Florida. Lizzie married Leroy Smucker and Lydia married Jonathan Lantz. They raised their families on local farms and both are now widows. (Stephen Lantz, Reuben's nephew, informed me Reuben died recently in an automobile accident.)

I do not remember my school days really well. I know I could not speak English when I started school. I do remember when I was in first grade sometimes the days were very long. I could see the clock from where I sat in the front row. I would watch the minute hand go ever so slow from 3:00 to 3:30. It seemed like forever. We were dismissed at 3:30.

My second grade teacher was Mildred Brackbill. I had perfect attendance that year, no-days missed- and I still have my perfect attendance certificate. Grades three through eight Miss Sadie Yost was my teacher. She lived in Buena Vista, the second house south of the school by the Pequea Creek.

Buena Vista was one of eleven one-room schools in Salisbury Township. The other schools were Limeville, Waterloo, White Horse, Buchland, Mount Airy, Whitehall, Spring Garden, Mt. Pleasant, Millwood, and Gap. Each year several of the four or five School Board Directors would visit the schools once or twice. Miss Yost, our teacher, would of course expect our best behavior and performance during these visits. This one visit, when I was in third grade, she had the first graders recite nursery rhymes they had memorized. The Directors chuckled a bit when Sarah Zook recited:

One two, buckle my shoe
Three four, make the door shut
Five six, pick up sticks
Seven eight, lay them straight
Nine ten a big fat hen

A rotating library of about twenty books was passed from one school to the next about every other month.. My brother John and I both enjoyed reading some of those books.

Recess was my favorite time of the school day, fifteen minute first recess, one hour lunch and fifteen minute second recess. We played games as cally over, red rover, bag tag, old gray wolf, softball and many others including fox and geese in winter time. When conditions were right in the winter arrangements were made to go off the school ground for sledding or skating. The two recesses were limited to five minute potty breaks then we had one and a half hour for our lunch break to sled or skate. That was lots of fun.

Sometimes during the winter when there were no outside activities some of us would bring a potato along in the morning, lay it on top of the furnace and have a delicious warm potato, with butter and salt for lunch. We had a Victrola at school and could enjoy listening to records while we ate. Our drinking water was brought over in a pail from across the road where Mary Lantz lived.

Usually immediately after lunch was a fifteen minute story time and Miss Yost would read a book. Next to recess this was my favorite time of the day. Several books I still remember are Heidi, Bambi and Hiawatha.

We boys liked to go to school barefooted, no shoes. One year we wanted to be like the Indians and get used to not wearing many clothes. A few of us boys wanted to see who of us could go the longest without shoes or a coat in the fall. One day my brother John and I went to school barefooted and no coats when in the afternoon it snowed. Dad came to school in his horse and carriage and brought us shoes, socks, and coats. We were embarrassed.

A rather humorous incident I remember from seventh grade was an answer I gave on a written geography test. The correct answer was Yarmouth. The best I could come up with was Yarface. The teacher laughed a bit but would not give me credit.

The summer between my seventh and eighth grade I had an accident at home on the farm. At that time we put wheat sheaves on shocks and later hauled the sheaves into the barn awaiting the thresher. I was the driver on top of a wagon load of sheaves going toward the barn on a slight downhill. As I pulled the reins to slow the horses the sheaves below me pushed out front, fell onto the back of the horses and I went with them. I rolled off the back of the lead horse and both front and back wheels, steel wheels, went over both my legs. Dr. Hostetter from White Horse came and after examination felt I had no broken bones. I had severe pain in my right knee and did not sleep that night. The next day I was admitted to the Lancaster General Hospital. There a stretcher was put on my right leg. The following day Dr. Atlee, my doctor, called Dad into a conference room and informed him they may have to amputate my leg. However, with no surgery and my knee on a stretcher for three weeks, it was healing and I came home.

A big surprise on my way home was how much the corn had grown in three weeks. While bedfast at home a visitor gave me the book, "The Way of a Man with a Maid." It was the first book I read on sex education and I still remember it. I was on crutches the rest of the summer but my knee healed.

Miss Yost had a radio at home so in the morning at school she informed us of any news of interest. Most of my school years were war years and I remember mostly her reports of World War II news, the advance of the allies, how many US soldiers lost their lives, etc. At home we were also very much aware of the war. Beginning in 1939 we participated in blackouts at designated times. All our windows had to be covered at night so no light could get through. This was in case of a bombing attack no targets would be visible. Various items were rationed because of scarcity. Gas and tires were major items rationed. These did not effect us so much because we had no car. Sugar, butter, coffee, meat and shoes were other major items that were scarce and could only be purchased with coupons. We were very aware of these shortages but "made do" and enjoyed life anyway.

Another effect of the war was that many young men were drafted, my older brother Seth among them. He served four years in Civilian Public Service, CPS, at various places including Terry,

Montana, Three Rivers, California and a camp in Maryland. He returned home when the war ended in 1945.

We had a sad Christmas vacation in 1941 when I was in seventh grade. At noon on the day before Christmas, Miss Yost responded to a knock on the door. She then told Christian and Melvin Lapp, brothers, to get their coats and belongings and go home with the person at the door. After they left she informed us their 16 year old brother Amos was killed in a farm accident at home. It was a different Christmas vacation.

I finished eighth grade in April 1943 when I was thirteen. However, we could get no permit to quit school before age fourteen. So I repeated eighth grade from the end of August till November 18, my birthday. Dad took me to Mr. Denlinger, a School Director near Gap and Mr. Denlinger signed and gave me a permit to quit school. It was a big day in my life. I was finished with school forever, I thought.

CHAPTER 3

Rumspringa

Turning sixteen is very significant if you are Amish. It is when you begin "running around" or rumspringa. I did not know much about rumspringa when I turned sixteen and was not real anxious to begin. Of the six or so major groups or gangs to join at sixteen I knew I would join the Groffies rather than the Amies, Mickeys or Keffers because most of the young people in Lower Pequea where I lived were in that gang. About five weeks after turning sixteen, I left home on a Sunday eve alone in my horse and buggy to see what rumspringa was like. I drove the ten miles to Intercourse where the Groffies met to find out where the singing is. The singing my first night was at a Zook farm along Route 340 on my way home. I was very curious to see what a singing was like. I had no friends at the singing but I knew a few people. Without friends singings weren't much fun. A few months after turning sixteen several other boys I knew turned sixteen and began coming to singings. We became good friends and I went every Sunday evening and began to enjoy it.

Sunday evening singings were held at homes where church services had been that day. The house or barn was thus prepared with tables and benches for the young people to meet and sing from the "Gesangbuch" in German. Average attendance was probably 50-100 young people. Most of the girls participated with singing, many of the boys didn't. After the singing there was often a square dance or hoe down for a short time before everyone went home.

Frequently at a singing a group of four or five boys would find a place in a barn or shed where they would have a case of beer. Occasionally they would be real "show offs" and everyone knew they had been drinking. Sometimes a group of boys would have a bottle of wine or whiskey which they shared among themselves. I was almost seventeen when I was first offered and accepted a drink by a few older boys. For about two years, ages seventeen and eighteen, I was frequently with a group that had something to drink.

Sometimes on a Saturday night someone would host a hoedown. This was usually when the parents were away from home. Square dancing with lively music was the feature of the evening. Drinking was more common at hoedowns than at singings. But the majority of the people just came to visit and be with friends.

Possibly the major social life for most of the youth is participating in a small group of eight to twelve or more that somehow develops. I was part of such a group for several years. We would meet on a Sunday afternoon or occasionally for a weekend. One of our group had a record player with a collection of many records. Often the main thing in our small group gathering was sitting around the record player, listening to the records, visiting and playing cards. Because girls were part of the small group there was usually no drinking.

I was probably seventeen when I drove the twelve miles to New Holland with a friend and saw my first movie. For a period of time then seeing a movie was an option for a Saturday night activity. The only movies I remember well are the Roy Rogers and Dale Evans movies.

I was aware of course that much of what I did was not approved of by my parents and actually forbidden by the church. But I did not particularly feel rebellious or carry much guilt. It's just what you did if you were an Amish teenager.

When I turned eighteen I was given a new buggy with a

horse by my parents. It was great to have my own horse and buggy even though it was a gift, not something I had purchased with my own money. Life was good!

Also now that I was eighteen my parents really felt I needed to join church. And it was okay with me. It was all a part of becoming an adult. So the summer of 1948, between spring communion in April and fall communion in October, I was with a group of about fifteen that met approximately twenty minutes with the preachers every Sunday we had church services (church services are held every other Sunday only). Just as the services began we filed into a separate room where the preachers were. We filed by age, boys first then girls. After being seated we were asked by the lead preacher what our desire (or request) was. The oldest boy answered, "My desire is to make peace with God and the church." The rest of us down the line by age, boys then girls, each answered, "My desire is the same." This in German, of course. Then we were given some instructions on what this required.

In October 1948 I was baptized with my friends by our bishop Sam Stoltzfus (Buck Sam) in Jonathan and Anna Lapp's wagon shed. I don't remember who the girls were. The boys by age were: Sam Fisher's Ben (Cactus), me, Aaron Beiler's Levi, Jake Zook's Christ, Sam Lapp's Christ, Levi Fisher's Amos, Gid Dienner's Gid and Elam Stolzfus' Melvin. As of this writing, May 2017, three of us boys are still living: Levi Beiler, Christ Zook, and I.

What did my baptism mean to me? It was not life changing. It was just the right thing to do. I knew it was because of Jesus that we would go to heaven when we die. And as an adult one needed to be baptized and a member of a church. I had met these requirements and felt okay.

The summer I was twenty my brother John, two years younger than I, left home unannounced, hitch-hiked to Ohio and got a job on a farm. When assured by Dad that he could live at home and have a car, he came home. Our neighbor, Phares Lantz, invited him to go along to Maple Grove Mennonite Church. John became a part of the young folks there and was baptized. John and I were close as brothers and talked a lot. Occasionally I went with him to special evening meetings at Maple Grove. We talked about salvation and I had many questions.

I'm not sure when I first began noticing five boys at singings who were often together and seemed a bit different. They were usually jolly but did not smoke, drink, hoe down or use foul language. I was ready for something different and began making friends with them. The boys were Joe Fisher, Stevie Esh, Jonathan Stoltzfus, or Brownie, Fred's Christ, or Dickie, and Fred's Freddie. Freddie was not a church member and had a car.

It was during this time that I heard a stirring message about hell given by David Miller from Oklahoma, an Amish evangelist. I did not have assurance of salvation. The Amish understood and taught one could have a living hope but not absolute assurance. For some months I lived in terror, not knowing if I would go to hell or heaven. I wished I had never been born. I prayed and prayed and read the Scriptures. One day up in the barn on the straw mow from my pocket New Testament I read 1 John 5:13, "I write these things to you who believe in the name of the Son of God, so that you may know that you have eternal life." Somehow there in the straw mow the Lord touched me, I received assurance and my life was changed. I was "born again"!

CHAPTER 4

The Group

During this time of change in my life I began to see much of what I had been participating in as displeasing to God, as sin. Thus most of my social life was now with the five boys previously mentioned including a few girls who also disapproved of much that took place at singings and hoedowns. We began getting together in each others' homes and with time had our own small group. Our group was noticeably different and drew some attention. We invited others to join us and occasionally some did, more girls than boys. Mary Ann Riehl was adopted as a baby by the Riehl sisters, three single Amish ladies. The Riehls lived very close to Lancaster Mennonite High School and Mary Ann graduated from there. Mary Ann wanted to be Amish but did not fit into Rumspringa. Thus she became a part of The Group. Mary Ann later received a BS in Nursing and taught at Lancaster General Hospital Nursing School as a single Old Order Amish woman the rest of her adult life.

"The Group" as we called ourselves was the major part of my social life ages twenty to twenty-five. I felt I was the leader of The Group for several years which gave me fulfillment and a ministry. At the beginning my role model was partially the Maple Grove Mennonite Church MYF which my brother John kept telling me about. Eventually our activities included prayer meetings and Bible studies. Many of the parents supported this and even attended. Others however, disapproved.

Over time we, that is the youth in The Group, found out about similar groups in other Amish communities: Stuarts Draft in Virginia, Holmes County Ohio, Nappanee and Goshen Indiana and Hutchinson, Kansas. We communicated by letter and a bit of back and forth visiting. In the summer of 1953 I was able to attend an Amish Conference and Youth Meeting in Hutchinson, Kansas that brought several hundred Amish youth and adults together. The Amish Church in Lancaster County did not approve of the meeting so I was not allowed to partake of communion that fall. But because no prior warning had been given I did not need to make a public confession of sin in the church.

For most of the years when I was ages twenty to twenty-five my parents hosted a German school Saturdays during the fall and winter. I taught grades five through eight. I also had a small bookstore open to the public in an upstairs room of our large farm house. I had books and tracts mostly from Moody Press but also Herald Press, Zondervan and Baker. I read a lot and was nurtured by conservative authors and theology. I had many church and theology discussions with my parents.

In January of 1952 Fred's Christ invited me to go with him to Northern Light Gospel Mission Bible School in Loman, Minnesota by International Falls. This was a wonderful trip for me. We went by Greyhound Bus. A scene I still remember, now sixty-five years later, is going north through Wisconsin seeing the farms, the snow and the round barns. It was an unforgettable experience.

This, being my first Bible School and having no Sunday School, meant much of the teaching was new to me. But I kept notes, which I still have, and tried to understand and remember. Some of my teachers were Andrew Glick and Eli Hochstetler from North Dakota, Lawrence Yoder, Llewellyn Groff and Bill Kurtz from Minnesota.

Three years later, January of 1955, Harvey Stoltzfus from

Morgantown took Fred's Christ and me for another three week term at Loman. This time we encountered the Holy Spirit revival that had taken place there, especially among some young people. Before arriving at Loman we stopped at Gerald Derstine's home at, I think, Strawberry Lake. There we observed as Gerald, Fred's Amos and several others, filled with the Holy Spirit, demonstrated some very unusual things for us. It was my first encounter with the Charismatic Renewal Movement.

The Group slowly became larger. We had what we considered good clean fun within an overall spiritual atmosphere. Among our activities we regularly sang for elderly people in their homes and in various group homes referred to as Old Peoples' Homes. When invited we gave Sunday evening programs at Beachy Amish and Mennonite Churches. One by one young people who wanted an alternative joined The Group, sometimes against their parents' wishes. The Brunk Revivals greatly influenced many in the group. Most parents and many adults approved of and supported The Group. However church leaders were very concerned and expressed their disapproval openly. In The Group we prayed for each other and earnestly sought God's guidance. The Group meant very much to me.

CHAPTER 5

Cattle Boat with Heifer Project

During World War II Dan West from Indiana was a relief worker in Europe for the Church of the Brethren. He saw great needs and proposed that rather than giving families milk they could give a heifer. Through his efforts and concerns Heifer Project was incorporated in 1944. Because no one was found to transport heifers across the ocean during the war, their first shipment was eighteen heifers to Puerto Rico in July 1944.

Following the shipment to Puerto Rico the Brethren Service Committee made arrangements with the United Nations Relief and Rehabilitation Administration, UNRRA, to transport animals for Heifer Project, mostly to Poland, Italy, Greece and Germany with a few trips to China, Belgium and Djibouti. They delivered mostly horses, heifers and mules but also some chicks, rabbits and goats. Around 7,000 men and boys ages 16-72 accompanied these animals on approximately 360 trips and 73 different ships. Luke Bomberger from New Holland, Pa. was the first of the many Mennonites that joined these "Seagoing Cowboys." Luke made nine trips as a "Cowboy", his first in 1945 when he was 17.

After UNRRA no longer provided transportation the program continued but the size and frequency of shipments decreased. Many shipments went to Japan. Special arrangements were made for heifers to be sent to Germany. The S.S. American Importer made a round trip from New York to Germany approximately every six weeks. One "hold" on the ship was reserved for cattle with the understanding Heifer Project would supply cattle for every trip and take care of them. That's where I came in.

In 1950 Leslie Yoder from Oregon, a field worker for Heifer Project, approached my dad about helping with Heifer Project. Leslie contacted farmers in southeastern Pennsylvania to donate heifers which they did. A place was needed to hold 20-25 heifers a few days before trucking them into Hoboken, NJ. Dad agreed to provide that need. So local farmers would bring their heifers to our farm. After all the heifers for a particular shipment arrived, Dr. Bryer, our veterinarian, made sure each heifer was with calf and healthy. Heifer Project was responsible for the heifers on the ship thus they had cowboys accompany them. Dad made arrangements that I could accompany a shipment.

On Wednesday morning October 22, 1952 I was accompanied by five of my buddies, Dickie, Brownie, Dudley, Ben and Freddie, with Freddie as driver, to Hoboken, New Jersey and the cattle boat. At Hoboken we had our good-byes and I met my fellow cowboy, Earl Woodard from Luray, Va. After the fifty-four heifers and one bull were loaded onto the S.S. American Importer, a freighter or cargo ship, Earl and I went on board and were informed of our responsibilities. We left by New York Harbor passing the Statue of Liberty. This of course was my first time on a ship and very exciting. Our cattle, in a small hold below deck, made up only a small part of the cargo. Most visible were the many army tanks and trucks and a few American cars on deck.

Although our ship was a freighter eight or nine passengers were on board. Earl and I got to especially know two of them, German boys being deported to Germany. They both had attempted to get into the United States without legal documents. Manford, a sailor, abandoned his ship in California and got caught about three months later. Gunter was a hide-away on a ship docking at New York but got caught at the dock. Both were being deported. We made our acquaintance the second day at sea already. They helped Earl and me with our chores and we had dinner together. Our third day at sea our first calf was born but did not survive. It was dumped into the ocean. Also we began experiencing rough sea. Everyone was assigned a life boat. Earl and I both experienced sea sickness and were sick until we reached the North Sea. Earl could not get out of bed for several days but the cattle had to be taken care of. Every morning and evening we needed to give them water, hay and grain and make sure they were bedded properly. I was not as sick as Earl but could only crawl on hands and knees on deck, I couldn't walk. The German boys, mostly Gunter, helped take care of the heifers. We had another heifer freshen and Gunter milked the two fresh heifers. The German boys did not experience any sea sickness. I made an entry into my diary every day and Gunter signed each entry- Gunter Karl Krausse, ge. 20-8-32- to affirm what I had written.

On Saturday November 1 we spotted land for the first time since leaving New York. Eventually I recognized the "The Cliffs of Dover" which for me was exciting. Going up the North Sea at night I could see lights from France, a wonderful scene. On Sunday November 2 late afternoon we picked up a local pilot who took us into Bremerhaven but no passengers got off. The cow that was fresh October 25 died and we had another fresh heifer. Monday at 2:00 still at Bremerhaven Earl and I were able to leave ship and go uptown. Before leaving we said good-bye to Gunter and Manford, our German friends, and were sad to see them leave with two policemen. Earl and I were asked to put a halter on each heifer to prepare for their unloading. On Wednesday November 5 we cruised up the Weser River approximately 40 miles arriving at Bremen our destination at 15:00 hours. Roy Schmidt from Heifer Project met us on the ship.

On Thursday morning a crew began unloading the heifers individually, each in a crate or box with a crane. At 10:00 there was a celebration and a party on board as the 1,000th heifer was unloaded from the S.S. American Importer. The heifer had a large good-will wreath around her and some VIPs enjoyed lunch on board in the dining room. The heifers were loaded on trucks and Earl and I were no longer responsible for them. Each heifer will find a home with a poor farmer selected by Heifer Project. This farmer agrees to give the first heifer calf of his heifer to another needy farmer.

From Bremen Earl and I went with Roy Schmidt and Mr. and Mrs. Ziegler to the Brethren Headquarters in Kassel where we stayed overnight. There was snow on the ground with beautiful winter scenery. Earl had been in Europe the previous year with Brethren Voluntary Service and now had a girlfriend living in the Schwartzwald in South Germany. He agreed that I could accompany him to visit her. So we traveled by train from Kassel in North Germany to Donaueschingen in South Germany with stopovers at Frankfort and several other places. The ground was covered with snow and the scenery was beautiful. We got a Gasthaus in Donaueschingen where we left our luggage and cleaned up with no hot water. Earl's girlfriend, Eleonore Behrenett, lived in the town of Neudingen nearby. Late afternoon Earl took the train to Eleonore's house and stayed overnight. I joined them for Sunday lunch and dinner. We spent the evening there playing games and singing before I returned to the Gasthause. I had a wonderful time with Earl and Eleonore going to several different villages on Monday. On Tuesday I went with Earl by train to see friends of his along the Bodensee or Lake Constance. At Konstang we took a ferry across the lake and stayed with Earl's friends. On Thursday we took the ferry back to Konstang where we got a train for Luzern. I was now in Switzerland, my favorite country since grade school mostly because of Heidi, a favorite book of mine. I was now in Heidi's country and saw her beautiful mountains. In Luzern we walked on the famous covered bridge over the lake. Earl had come to Luzern partially to take the cog rail up Mt. Rigi.

On Friday we took a small boat from Luzern to Vitznau and got the cog train to the top of Mount Rigi, a wonderful experience. It was my first time seeing people skiing as we saw them from the cog train.

From Luzern Earl returned to Eleonore's home and I took a train for Basel. Mennonite Central Committee, MCC, has an office in Basel and I had given this as an address for mail from home. So I was anxious to get there. I thought with my Pennsylvania Dutch background I knew a good bit of German but I had a major lesson to learn at Basel. After leaving the Banhof I approached a policeman and asked if he could tell me how to get to the address I had for MCC. I said, "Kanst du mir sagen wo...?" "Can you tell me where...?" He responded angrily and told me, "Hier sagt Mann nicht 'Kanst du.'" "Here one does not say, 'Kannst du'". I don't know how I traveled this far in Germany and was unfamiliar with the polite form of German. The polite form is always used with strangers and especially with anyone in position of authority as a policeman. I should have said, "Kennen Sie mir sagen wo...?" I'm not sure I used the word "Bitte" or "Please" which is always included in German in such a request. The policeman was very displeased and unhappy by the way I addressed him but he did tell me how to get to MCC Headquarters.

I received a royal welcome at MCC, an Amish boy from Pennsylvania traveling alone. Among others I met John Hostetler, a young single man from Ohio, who had just begun working at MCC, Basel, six weeks earlier. I went with him half a day contacting various homes. John could speak some German but in his introduction he always asked, "Sprechen Sie English?" "Do you speak English?" John later married a German speaking girl, Katherine Penner, and worked for MCC until his retirement. Now at age 91, he still volunteers regularly at Book Savers in Ephrata, PA. I also received three or four very welcome letters from family and friends here.

Another person I met at MCC, Basel, was Dora Lichty. Dora informed me an Amish boy was in the Pax unit in Bachnang, Germany. I thought that was doubtful as I didn't think it would be possible for an Old Order horse and buggy Amish boy as I was to be in Pax. I was very curious. My next destination was Kassel. Bachnang would not be much out of the way. I decided to satisfy my curiosity.

A few days later in the evening after dark I was standing on the porch of a house in Bachnang holding my suitcase and peering in the window. I saw eight or ten young men sitting around a table eating supper. I figured I was at the right place and knocked on the door. I was invited in and had supper with them. I discovered Simon Miller from Iowa was one of the boys and he was Amish. I spent the next day on the project with Simon and got to know him. I also got to know John Mark King from Wisconsin, Pax Pastor Jesse Short and Nelson Waybill with whom I worked under Mennonite Publishing House many years later. Simon later was transferred to Greece where in the summer of 1954 he and another Pax boy, Eli Miller, drowned in a lake while swimming.

At Bachnang Simon saw me off as I boarded the train for Kassel. Arriving at Kassel I had four or five letters waiting for me. There I also met Earl again and Roy Schmidt. The three of us went to Koblentz in a VW where we met some of the farmers who were just now receiving their heifers. The next day we drove back to Kassel and I got the train for Hamburg. I left for home from Hamburg on the Elbe River on the S.S. American Clipper, a freighter similar to the S.S. American Importer. The arrangement at that time was that cowboys accompanying heifers on the S.S. American Importer every six weeks did not get paid cash but received a round trip ticket good for one year on any freighter owned by the United

States line. I had an enjoyable trip coming home making friends with various people. I only had a touch of seasickness, nothing serious. About three days before New York we encountered a major storm. The waves were higher than the ship. I assumed we might not make it through but we did. In the evening of December 3 the lights of New York City looked very welcoming. I said good-bye to various passengers and embarked around 7:30. I got a taxi to the bus depot, got a Greyhound and arrived at Ben Beilers, my sister Lena, along Route 30 at 2:00 am Thursday morning. This trip was probably life-changing for me in that I was introduced to Pax.

FOOTNOTE: Much of the information about Heifer Project and seagoing cowboys was obtained from Peggy Reiff Miller, Goshen, Indiana. Peggy is the author of the book THE SEAGOING COWBOY.

CHAPTER 6

Pax

When I turned 21 Dad was ready to turn the farm work over to me so he could partially retire. So in the spring of 1951 I began farming on shares. Dad owned the farm, the equipment and the cattle. I was responsible for all the labor and one-third of the expenses. I received one-third of the profit including one-third of the calves. We had 24 milking cows. My brother John worked for me as a hired man. We both lived at home and may have had free board and lodging, I don't remember. This arrangement worked very well until I went to Pax and was profitable for everyone.

My social life was pretty much with "The Group". Aden Gingerich, an Amish boy from Plain City, Ohio, was at Lancaster Mennonite High School in 1952-53. Because of Aden I got to travel to Plain City several times and got to know many of the Amish young people there. In December 1952 two car loads of us young folks went to Indiana to the wedding of Harvey Graber and Miriam Hochstetler. I was table-waiter. In August of 1953 a few of us young folks from here attended the Amish Youth Conference in Hutchinson, Kansas that I referred to in my chapter on The Group. On our way home from Kansas we spent several days in Kalona, Iowa and among others visited Simon Miller's parents and Simon's fiancee, Beth Beachy. I had visited Simon in Bachnang, Germany on my cattle boat trip. In November 1954 a car load of us Amish young folks went to Plain City then to Holmes County, Ohio. Mary Fisher was with us and wanted to see her "Words of

Cheer" pen pal Sara Ellen Miller whom she had never met. So on a Monday morning we stopped at Abe Millers and briefly met Sara Ellen. Sometime later I got to know Sara Ellen much better! In January of 1955 I attended Northern Light Gospel Mission three week Bible School which I had attended in 1952 also. George Beiler and Homer Coblentz did the chores while I was gone.

So I did a little traveling in the few years I was farming but most of the time I was at home working. The cows needed to be milked every morning and evening and we had 80 acres to farm with horses. We had no electricity or telephone. John and I enjoyed our work but I was a little restless. Sometime before my cattle boat trip I had read a book published by Herald Press giving an account of MCC relief workers in Europe shortly after the war. Among the workers were two Amish boys from Kansas. I thought now there is something I could do and I think I would enjoy it. Then on the cattle boat trip I met Simon Miller in Pax. Thus in the spring of 1954 I informed my parents I would like to serve in Pax. They of course were not thrilled about it but when they realized how serious I was they agreed to make arrangements that I could go. In July we saw in "the Budget" that Simon and Eli Miller drowned while swimming in Greece. Mother and Dad thought I would change my mind about going, but I didn't. To my surprise Dad said he would sell the farm if I leave. Samuel Beiler bought the farm and the cows. We had implement and household sale Saturday December 11, 1954. It was rather hard for me to leave "The Group" my social life and my parents, Dad was 70, but I felt it was God's will and the right thing for me to do.

Because I quit farming I lost my "farm deferment" status which gave me the right to work on a farm rather than being drafted into the military. I was approved as a "Conscientious Objector" to the military and given approval to serve in alternative service under MCC. My alternative service officially began March 22, 1955, the day my orientation began at MCC in Akron, PA. I had said good-bye to various people but my final good-byes were at Hoboken, NJ, Wednesday March 30, 1955. My parents and more than 20 friends and family members were there to say their final good-byes.

What is Pax? Following World War II much of western Europe was in devastation, particularly the countries of Belgium, France, Italy, the Netherlands, and Germany. Among this rubble there were thousands of Russian and Prussian Mennonite refugees who were now living in refugee camps in Germany. Resources were found to provide land and materials to build homes for many of them but the refugees would need to come up with 10% of the cost. MCC agreed to provide the 10% by doing the labor to build the homes. Thus on April 6, 1951, twenty young American farm boys arrived on the shores of Europe, the beginning of Pax.

PAX GERMANY

On March 30, 1955, nine boys were really wondering what Pax is like. They were Carl Beyeler, Henry Gehman, Ernest Geiser, Arlin Hunsberger, Norman Kennel, Omar Lapp, Roger Nofziger, Jim Short and Roy Voth. We nine boys were on the Grote Beer, a Dutch ship, leaving home for two years to serve in Pax. I was 25, the others were 19-21 years of age. It seemed like a big commitment, not knowing if we would ever come home again. On the ocean we all experienced some seasickness. We had devotions together every morning and were learning to know each other. Beginning about the fifth day out we had German classes with a teacher from Venezuela for several days. With only 117 passengers we were not crowded as the Grote Beer had capacity for 850 passengers. On Friday, April 8, in the morning we docked at Rotterdam. Charles Yoder and two other MCC men met us and took us to MCC Headquarters in Amsterdam. At Amsterdam we went downtown on our own. Carl Beyeler got on the wrong bus to return to MCC, had no address with him, but was finally brought home late at night by two policemen.

After touring Holland several days we headed for Frankfurt, Germany, seeing the Rhine River and climbing the Cologne Cathedral on the way. At MCC Headquarters in Frankfurt we were introduced to what we should expect in Pax and were assigned to our units. Henry Gehman, Roger Nofziger and I were to be at the Enkenbach Unit, the other six were assigned to the Bachnang Unit. Several Pax men were at Frankfurt when we arrived and I was especially surprised as I met one of them. I learned he was from Pennsylvania as I was, from Lancaster County and sure enough from Gap, same as I. It was Bob Weaver. We lived only a mile apart and had never met. He was Mennonite and I was Amish and our paths had just never crossed.

At Enkenbach homes were being built for German Mennonite refugees from Prussia, mostly widows, children and grandparents. When Henry, Roger, and I arrived three houses were finished and occupied. The Pax boys lived in a section of the first house. Four families lived in each completed house. Our introductory work was being a "handlanger", "mudboy" and digging a nine foot deep hole, six foot in diameter, for a septic tank, mostly through sandstone. We got blisters and were very tired at the end of the day. The three of us joined the seven already working there and were well received. By signing a fake carbon copy I promised to do the dishes for a week soon after I arrived. Enkenbach is in the Palatinate, or Pfalz, section of Germany. Pennsylvania Dutch, my first language, is a Palatinate dialect which was helpful for me. However the refugees living in the homes we built were not from the Palatinate so my Pennsylvania Dutch was not so helpful. One day it was raining lightly and I was walking with one of the grandfathers living there. I commented in Pennsylvania Dutch "It's raining". He could not understand what I was saying. It was embarrassing.

I was at Enkenbach five months and enjoyed it. I adjusted and learned many things. Margaret Martin from Ephrata, Pa, a plain Mennonite lady, was our matron and helped me feel at home. I helped Truman Hertzler lay bathroom tile, did some regular block laying and got accustomed to the work and our work schedule. I was introduced to ping pong. I learned how to "horse and goggle" a method of deciding who gets the one piece of pie left over. In May when LaMar Stauffer went to Greece I bought his bike and thus had a means of transportation. One weekend some of us had a boat ride on the Rhine River from Bingen to Koblentz and back which I greatly enjoyed. I also enjoyed going to Mennonite youth gatherings at various places over the weekends, sometimes with Milton Harder, our Pax Pastor. A weekend in June all of us went to Mannheim to hear Billy Graham which was a great experience. I think there were 20,000 people there. Billy had a wonderful interpreter who would use the same emotions and hand-expressions while repeating Billy's message in German. Many of us understood the German and the English. In July Susan Weaver from Terre Hill, Lancaster County, Pa, joined us for six weeks and helped work on the houses. A very sad experience that touched us was when in August Widow Thimm's son Hans and his fiancee were killed in an automobile accident. Hans was a brother to Arno Thimm who later graduated from Eastern Mennonite College. I enjoyed attending the worship service the refugees held in the Altersheim, or Old Peoples Home. I especially enjoyed their hearty singing. I brought home one of their hymnals.

By mid July six houses were finished and occupied and two more were almost finished. Each house had four families in it with four rooms and a bath for each. A wall was in the middle, two families at each end, one upstairs and one downstairs. Later a total of fifteen four-family homes plus some one family homes were completed. And a church building was put up with Albert Keim as project foreman.

I stayed in touch with my home community by writing and receiving letters. I wrote home every week and had a letter from Mom or Dad every week. I still have those letters today. I also received letters regularly from someone in "The Group" and I received "the Budget" a mostly Amish publication, every week. I submitted several letters to the Budget that were published.

In late July Dwight Wiebe, our Pax Director, interviewed me about going to Greece in August and asked me to go. I would have preferred to stay in Germany. I knew almost nothing about Greece. But Dwight presented the need and I felt God was asking me to go so I said, "Yes, I will go to Greece for two years".

PAX GREECE

It was with some sadness that I said good-bye to my friends at Enkenbach, both my German friends and my fellow Paxers. And I had almost no idea what Greece might be like. John Hostetler from MCC and LaMarr Kopp, director of European Mennonite Voluntary Service, both stationed in Europe, had business interests in Belgrade and in Greece that they wanted to investigate. I needed transportation to Greece so the three of us left Germany August 27 in a VW Bug. We stopped in Zurich, Switzerland to get visas for Yugoslavia, went through the Brenner Pass and the Swiss and Austrian Alps into Yugoslavia. Yugoslavia did not have many automobiles at that time and from Belgrade south to Greece hardly any paved roads, only gravel and dirt roads. The main traffic was ox carts, horse drawn vehicles, bicycles, and people walking. In a letter home I wrote "This is the most interesting and enjoyable trip I ever took."

My new home in Village Tsakones was upstairs in a two story mud brick house owned by "Grandpa and Grandma", an elderly progressive village couple. Four "old" Pax boys, Larry Eisenbeis from South Dakota, Harley Good from Virginia, Ralph Shelly

Nine boys leaving for a two year VS term in Pax in March 1955. Henry Gehman, Arlin Hunsberger, Jim Short, Roy Voth, Ernest Geiser, Norman Kennel, Roger Nofziger, Carl Beyeler, and Omar Lapp.

The houses built by Pax boys in Enkenbach, Germany. Susan Weaver, La Moine Epp, Wilson Myers, Cal Graber, and Henry Gehman.

Stacking brick. Roger Nofziger and Omar Lapp.

Omar at Enkenbach.

Sofula (Sophie) Papadapoulos with her father in Tsakones, Greece. Sophie is now the wife of Gerald (Shorty) Jantzi. The tree by the wagon is for silk worms.

The village store in Tsakones with Yorgo, the owner, and his wife.

Omar, with hat, and Luke Martin threshing beans. The chicken house we Pax boys built is on the left. The house we lived in is on the right.

Omar getting sod or mud brick he cut to be used in building the chicken house.

The four Pax boys in Tsakones showing their projects. LaMar Stauffer, Dick Lambright, Omar Lapp, Arlin Hunsberger with Christos their interpreter in overcoat and Apostilidies, their landlord.

Fotie, a friend of the Pax boys, very pleased with his hybrid corn.

Paul Kraybill and Orie Miller on an official visit to the Greek MCC Pax units.

Omar Lapp, Dick Lambright, Arlin Hunsberger and LaMar Stauffer on a Sunday outing with Nettie their donkey.

The Pax units Tsakones and Panayitsa 1956: LaMar Stauffer, Dick Lambright, Omar Lapp, Jim Lambright, Ann Ewert, Arlin Hunsberger, Bob Stauffer, Donald Schierling (Scuff), John Hiebert, John Jantzen, Norman Kennel, and Alex Mavrides.

from Quakertown, Pa. and Dean Zehr from Illinois, all from Village Tsakones along with Denzel Short from Michigan, now from Panayitsa, were leaving for home in a week or so. LaMar Stauffer from Lancaster, Pa, had arrived in May and Arlin Hunsberger from Telford, Pa. had just arrived. One of the things the "old" Pax boys did while still with us was take me to Edessa, our nearest large town along a main highway and introduce me to a restaurant meal. They gave me a very popular and one of the best Greek desserts, a peach in yogurt. I had never heard of yogurt and almost could not eat it, to their delight.

Our village of about 50 families was a typical farm village in the Aridea Valley, Nomis Pellis, Macedonia in northern Greece. Everyone in Greece lives in a village, town or city. There are no individual homes scattered throughout the countryside. The villages have no paved roads, no electricity, no automobiles, usually no bicycles, sometimes one phone in a coffee shop. The fields are scattered often a half hour or more away from the village.

Following World War II the people in northern Greece were divided to whom they should associate and work with, Yugoslavia and communists, their neighbors, or the Allies in western Europe. So for several years a guerrilla warfare was happening and it was not safe for families to stay in their villages. They temporarily went to large towns or cities for safety. When they finally returned many fields were overgrown with tall grass, weeds and briers and could not be plowed with their implements. MCC was invited to bring a small tractor to break up the fields which they did. The villagers' farm implements were primitive, drawn by cows, oxen or for the more well to do farmer, one horse or one mule. After the overgrown fields were plowed once with the tractor the villagers could again farm them.

When I arrived the Pax Unit in Tsakones had rented about four acres, not all together, on which we did out experimental farming. We also worked with introducing canning and working with chickens, turkeys and hogs. My job was to continue with experimental crops, especially introducing hybrid seed corn. Arlin Hunsberger worked with canning and LaMar worked with chickens. Of course we helped each other. And we had a Greek interpreter, Christos, living with us. One of the first days I was in Greece I was working by myself in one of our fields. Sophie Papadapoulos, a 14 year old girl, and her father were in their field just beside ours and came over to welcome me, a new Pax boy. I did not know one Greek word so our communication was quite limited and embarrassing. Later Sophie married a Pax boy.

To me it seemed there was a much greater difference between Germany and Greece than between home and Germany. But after a month or so I enjoyed living in Tsakones, Greece more than in Enkenbach, Germany. Probably what I missed most from Germany were the "Jugend Treffen" or German Young Peoples meetings that I frequently was able to attend. In Germany the work was very structured. We were told what to do. In Greece we were pretty much on our own and decided what to do and when. One of my lowest times in Greece was after being there about three months and not being able to learn the language. I had memorized possibly about 50 Greek words but I was not able to understand what a person was saying or have a conversation in Greek. I thought possibly I was too dumb to learn Greek and I had almost two more years before I could go home. I was depressed. However in another month I was beginning to pick up words and phrases and lo and behold within a year I was able to communicate in Greek fairly well.

Another negative experience was soon after I arrived and the first time I attended the Greek Orthodox Church. I of course understood no Greek nor had I ever attended a liturgical service as Episcopalian or even Lutheran. To me the service appeared pagan, the kissing of pictures, the incense, the chanting. I thought if ever I saw idolatry, this is it. However, either the church changed or I changed. Two years later before leaving for Western Europe and home I recall I had an unusually meaningful worship experience in the Greek Church one Sunday. And I had various good worship times in the church previously. So something had changed. I now understood the phrase, "Kyrie eleison", "Lord have mercy".

According to my diary and letters we were very busy all the time I was in Greece. For my first four months there were only three of us Paxers in Tsakones, LaMar Stauffer from Lancaster Pa, Arlin Hunsberger from Telford, Pa and I. Our interpreter, Christos, lived with us. Our work included seven half-acre or more scattered fields in which we experimented with corn, beans, cotton, oats, wheat, peas, alfalfa, irrigation, and fertilizer. And we tried to find ways villagers could preserve their many fruits and vegetables such as grapes, apples, peaches, tomatoes, eggplant, okra, plums, pears, as well as their meat when they butchered. We helped them make their raising of chickens, turkeys and hogs more profitable. We built our own rather large chicken house, a smaller turkey house and hog pen and an incubator room. We cut our own mud brick and cut down several trees for lumber. We hired a Greek foreman to help us build our chicken house. Dick Lambright from Indiana joined the three of us in November. We of course made our own meals, did our laundry and housekeeping. Almost every evening we had villagers visiting us. Three of us, Arlin, Dick and I decided to take a two week vacation in the winter when there was the least work. We planned a trip to Palestine. Dick's twin brother Bob was serving in Pax at a Brethren unit in Ioannia, Greece, and would go with us.

PALESTINE TOUR

At noon Monday, January 9, 1956, Arlin Hunsberger and I got the train at Thessalonica and arrived in Athens at midnight. In Athens we met Dick and Bob Lambright. Tuesday and Wednesday we got our visas for Egypt and Lebanon and all our plane and boat tickets. We had some difficulty getting through customs Wednesday afternoon but at 4:00 we got on our ship heading for Alexandria, Egypt. In fact our day was so busy we had not eaten anything all day. One of us bought a box of cookies as we were boarding. We were informed that with our 4th class tickets we could get no meals on board and would need to sleep on the deck. Neither proved to be true.

We had a nice cruise on the Mediterranean Sea, passing Crete and arriving at Alexandria Friday evening at 8:30. This was our first view of Africa and it was beautiful, palm trees, palaces and sailing boats. We got our money exchanged for Egyptian money and had many offers for help, were overcharged, and by the time we arrived in Cairo did not have enough money to buy tickets to Assuit. So we jumped on a 3rd class train without tickets and were on our way. We had been advised not to travel 3rd class but here we were, people standing, sitting on the dirty floor, jumping off while the train was running, etc. We rode along the Nile and saw lots of camels, donkeys, and water buffalo. Our reason for coming to Assuit was to meet Paul Peachey, a nephew of Shem Peachey and a friend of Arlin Hunsberger. Paul was in Pax at an American College farm in work similar to ours. We also toured the Lillian Trasher Orphanage, an outstanding orphanage with over 900 orphans from birth to 16.

From Assuit we went 200 some miles south by train along the Nile to Luxor, ancient Thebes. We explored several of the marvelous tombs of the Pharaohs, including the one that oppressed the Children of Israel. On our return north we spent a day with Paul Peachey at Assuit and he accompanied us to Cairo where we all enjoyed a camel ride, the pyramids, and the sphinx. Taking off for Beirut from Cairo we saw Port Said, the Suez Canal and the Mediterranean Sea from the air, all wonderful to behold.

Now we were in Palestine. We usually traveled by bus or public taxi, a vehicle that generally held six to twelve people and when they had a load they left for your destination. From Beiruit we took a bus trip to Tyre and Sidon then to Damascus by way of Baalbek. We spent a day and night in Damascus where we bought souvenirs, saw the street called Straight and the old city wall. We spent a night and part of a day at Amman then came to Jericho. Toured Jericho, swam in the Dead Sea and came to Jerusalem and Bethany. Among other things we saw Hezekiah's tunnel, the Garden of Gethsemane, the home of Mary and Martha and Lazarus' tomb. On Monday we visited the Stoltzfus twin sisters from Morgantown, Pa. who were beginning an orphanage in Hebron which is still in operation today. Near Bethlehem we saw the fields of Boaz and the shepherds' fields. We spent a day visiting Samaria, Bethel, Shechem, etc. Had a drink of water from Jacob's well.

On Wednesday January 25 G. Irvin Lehman helped us get our passports stamped so we could get into Israel. We had first met Irvin in Jericho and he had been a great help for us. Now we walked through "No Man's Land" into Israel. Our first night there we spent with Roy Kreiders. We took a three day trip to Galilee and back and saw most of the places mentioned in the Bible from this area including Haifa, Mt. Tabor, Capernaum, Nazareth, Caesarea, a 2 ½ hour boat ride on the Sea of Galilee and visited a Kibbutz. In Joppa we saw the house of Simon the Tanner and of Dorcas. We had a hotel room in Tel Aviv, near Joppa, and left from the Lydda airport at 12:00 noon on Sunday. Our flight went to New York City, but we got off at Athens and went back home to our villages where there was work for us.

PAX GREECE CONTINUED

My most enjoyable work in Greece was introducing hybrid seed corn in our village of Tsakones and surrounding villages. Native corn with irrigation had a top yield of about 35 bushels per acre. On our experimental plots with hybrid corn after three years we had 80 bushels to the acre. We had used cover crops and fertilizer as well as irrigation. The villagers of course saw our good production and beautiful ears. A major drawback for them was they could not use their own corn as seed. They needed to borrow money from the bank for seed and fertilizer. Some took the risk.

I made arrangements with various villagers that we would measure off one stremma, ¼ acre. I would plant half of it, furnishing the hybrid seed and fertilizer. They would plant the other half with native corn and we would compare the results. Except for working up the ground everything was done by hand. In good soil with fertilizer and irrigation for both, hybrid always did better, occasionally double. However on poor or sandy soil without irrigation native corn often did better than hybrid and had filled out ears where hybrid had many nubbins. My second year in Greece, the spring of 1957, I had experimental plots in six or eight surrounding villages as well as in our own village. Our interpreter would usually go with me in the Jeep for the first contact. I knew the language well enough that following the first contact I would go by myself. Some of the roads were hardly passable for motor vehicles, even our Jeep. When our Jeep was not available I went by bike or donkey. We three boys had bought a donkey. Usually no one in the village had ever tried hybrid. The spring of 1957, my final year in Greece, over half of the farmers in our village of Tsakones planted hybrid seed corn because of these experiments. Usually it did very well. The villagers had no way of preserving their fruits and vegetables. They sold what they could at market in the town of Aridea, about a 45 minute walk. The Pax boys prior to us had introduced canning in glass jars which they liked. However jars were expensive, breakable, hard to get and sometimes not a very good quality. Arlin Hunsberger kept up the interest in canning. He found out good tin cans were available in Thessalonica and not expensive. Because of the great interest in canning a central place was needed to do the work. Arlin was aware of a good empty brick building in our neighbor village Rothonia and made arrangements to rent it. Rothonia was only a short walk away and considered our home village as well as Tsakones. Some of our best friends and supporters lived in Rothonia. Eventually Arlin bought a sealer and set it up in the building. Almost everyone cooperated and the cannery was a central meeting place. All the fruits and vegetables not sold at market were canned. One day over 800 cans were canned, mostly peaches. In the summer of 1957 over 4,000 cans were sealed. As a result of this there is a successful commercial cannery in Rothonia today.

LaMar Stauffer was assigned the responsibility of working with chickens. Nearly every family had several chickens running around that provided a few eggs and eventually meat. But LaMar and the Pax boys knew by experience that chickens could provide some income which the villagers greatly needed. As an experiment LaMar had villagers agree to provide adequate space and feed and care for 12-15 chickens according to his instruction. Great results came from this beginning. LaMar got a kerosene operated incubator and provided chicks for villagers that took care of them under his supervision. The year after LaMar left we had 2,000 eggs on our kerosene operated incubator that needed to be turned twice a day by hand. Today there are a number of large, well kept chicken houses in Tsakones.

The Pax Greece program began in Panayista in 1953. Panayitsa is a mountain village while Tsakones is in a valley. The villages are about 2 hours apart by Jeep going a long way around the mountains and about a seven hour walk directly over the mountains which we sometimes did. Whoever was unit leader for Greece lived in Panayitsa as did our lead interpreter Alex Maverides. A major project for Panayitsa was bringing over 20 Brown Swiss heifers from the States in the spring of 1956. In February five Pax boys from Germany came to build a barn for the heifers, Luke Martin,

Vernice Bixler, Chester Kurtz, Bob Stauffer, and Lowell Klassen. Ben Stauffer from Lancaster, Pa, father of Paxers Bob and LaMar, took major responsibility for financing and purchasing the cattle. The heifers came from Wisconsin. On May 9 a ceremony was held in Panayitsa for the arrival and distribution of the heifers. It was a great day. After the heifers freshened a challenge was how to market the extra milk with no refrigeration. Arrangements were made to sell the fresh milk every morning to families in Edessa. The Brown Swiss ate a lot and Panayitsa had no pasture. So all the cows were taken up in the mountains where there was pasture. A Pax boy and a Greek milked them there and sent the milk to Edessa. Unfortunately, there were too many challenges and the program did not continue.

We socialized with the villagers in various ways. One way was participating in Name Days. Greeks do not observe birthdays and when we were there many older people had no idea how old they were. When asked their age they just said, "many years". Greeks all have the name of someone in the Bible or a Saint. The day a Bible person or Saint is officially honored or remembered, everyone with that name celebrates by opening his or her home to visitors. We often participated in this. All visitors were treated with Greek sweets which I never learned to like.

The major pastime for young people was to walk back and forth through the village usually in groups of three to six. Eventually everyone gathers at an open spot in the village and the Greek dancing begins with a caller and music. It can get rather loud but seems to be lots of fun. Of course almost all of us Pax guys came with the assumption that all dancing was wrong and perhaps sinful. But we weren't so sure anymore. We usually just observed but sometimes we participated to their delight.

Our house was an open house considered public by the villagers. They felt comfortable just walking in which they did. We had visitors almost every evening. They came with questions, to play games, to learn English words or just to talk. Many times it was 9:00 or later till everyone left. One day we counted 23 visitors.

We also went to the coffee shop frequently. Every Greek village has one or two coffee shops that are well attended. In the summer at noon from about 11:00-4:00 no work is done in the fields because of the heat. Every man goes to the coffee shop at least once a day to get the latest news and gossip and perhaps a cup of coffee or some ouzo, their alcoholic drink. Women are seldom seen in the coffee shop. We went for our haircuts, sometimes a shave, but also just to say hello and have a cup of Greek coffee. We did not stay hours as many of the men did and we did not drink ouzo although most of us were somehow persuaded to taste it. We sometimes attended the Greek church but not regularly.

The two years I was in Greece I had the opportunity to travel back to Germany and Holland once to attend the MCC conference in Friedesheim, Holland. Many Paxers were there. We heard speakers such as H. S. Bender, Brother Cornelius Wall, Albert Myers, and Paul Bender. We all participated in communion. We of course visited nearby Witmarsum where Menno Simons preached. After the conference our car load, consisting of Donald Schierling (Scuff), Dick Lambright, Arlin Hunsberger, Norman Kennel, Luke Martin and me spent several days in Germany, mostly at Kaiserslautern. We got to visit the Enkenbach unit and I visited Omar Lantz, a former Amish boy with whom I went to school, now in the army at Landstuhl, near Enkenbach. We stopped at Bachnang on our way back. Our vehicle gave us many problems but eventually we got back to Greece. Except Luke Martin who stayed in Germany.

I also made a few long weekend trips with some of the others. In September Donald Schierling, LaMar Stauffer, Bob Stauffer, John Jantzen and I took a trip through Greece, including Berea, Delphi, Athens, Corinth, Sparta, Olympia, Patras, Ioannia and the

Greek monasteries at Megalopolia. It was an educational and enjoyable trip.

In January of 1957 Arlin Hunsberger, Norman Kennel, Alex
Mavrides and I set out for Mt. Athos, the monastery peninsula
for males only, no females. However our vehicle broke down on
a mountain top on a seldom traveled road. According to the map
we had there was a town several miles ahead of us. It was dusk
but Norman Kennel and I walked almost two hours to the town
and got help. It took two days to get our vehicle going again. We
three Paxers then toured Mt. Athos while Alex stayed with a friend.
There are 20 monasteries on Mt. Athos, many built on cliffs, mostly built in the sixteenth and seventeenth centuries. We were aware
someone from Aridea was a monk in residence there and we got to
visit with him. I had the unusual experience of being considered a
worldly person visiting a religious community just the opposite of
at home in my Amish community having worldly people visit us.
We stopped at Philippi on our way home.

Jim Lambright wanted to visit Istanbul before he went home
so John Wenger, Arlin Hunsberger and I accompanied him for a
long weekend trip. This was my only visit to Turkey. In our guided
tour we saw St. Sophia Church, Blue Mosque, etc. And on our own
drove up to the Black Sea. We again stopped at Philippi.

There is a Protestant church at Katerina with a membership
of 2,500. In the 1950s it was estimated there were between 8,000
to 10,000 Protestants in Greece. Greece had a total population of
about 8 million. Katerina is about 125 miles from Tsakones and I
with others got to attend church there three or four times.

We were privileged to have Orie Miller and Paul Kraybill,
representing Mennonite Central Committee and Eastern Mennonite Board of Missions, visit us in July of 1956. I gave them a tour
of some of our scattered field experiments and they asked many
questions. They checked out everything we did. I was aware they

both had a lot of experience and wisdom. They were basically observing to see if our project was worth supporting. I don't remember if they had any advice for us but I appreciated their visit.

A great event for the good happened at our unit in Tsakones in September 1956. Ann Ewert, originally from Minnesota, came to be our matron! It's remarkable the difference it made to have a woman present. Ann was a resourceful person and not only made a great contribution to our unit but also to the women and girls of the villages we worked in. Thank you, Ann. Ann turned 100 a year or so ago and I think she is still living.

The following is an event I took some pride in. By appointment I met with a farmer in Crisa, a nearby village, in his field. For some reason we did not have many contacts with the Crisa villagers. I had walked through the village to get to his field. After finishing my time with the farmer many villagers were returning home from their fields. We walked together for 15 or 20 minutes and leaving Crisa I was alone. I had chatted with a number of them and no one was aware I was an American, not a villager from Tsakones. Actually ever since I was in Greece I was frequently taken for a Greek, not an American, but usually my speech gave me away. My everyday clothes I had brought from home wore out soon after I was in Greece and I bought Greek everyday clothes. Also I did not have a short haircut like most of the Pax boys. I chalked it up as a plus that no one I talked with detected I was not a Greek.

The time came for me to leave Greece. It had become my home away from home. I enjoyed my work, I loved the people and I had many friends. Gerald Jantzi, Shorty, from Nebraska came to take my place and Harry Zimmerman from Pennsylvania came to take Arlin Hunsberger's place who was also leaving. Arlin left a few days before I did. The evening before I left a lot of villagers came to bid me farewell. We knew it was very possible we would never see each other again. Little did we realize I would be back in six months on my way home or that Sophie would become the wife of Shorty Jantzi and we would see each other occasionally in the States. I did not get to bed until 3:30 and I got up at 5:00 to be on my way to Thessalonica where I would get the train for Salzburg, Austria and International Work Camp. My time in Pax Greece was done.

WORKCAMP, MENNONITE WORLD CONFERENCE

I had an interesting, enjoyable trip on the Balkan Express through Yugoslavia to Salzburg, Austria. Long distant passenger trains in Europe had compartments for six or eight people facing each other. Leaving Thessalonica there were several Greek men and women, a German lady and I in our compartment. Soon after entering Yugoslavia two local girls joined us who could speak English. It so happened that I was the only one in our compartment that could converse with everyone and I did a lot of translating. I was in my glory.

LaMarr Kopp was director of International Work Camp in Europe and he asked me to be project foreman at Elixhausen, Austria, near Salzburg. The work was somewhat similar to the work at Enkenbach and the other German Pax units, building houses for refugees. Eleven girls and eight boys from nine different countries participated, mostly European but including Syria and Vietnam. Some of them hitchhiked all the way from their home including Albert Joelson from Sweden. Shirley Stauffer from Lancaster County was a participant. Tineka Nauta from Holland was camp leader. We actually worked very hard but did have some difficulty in working together well. We took turns in leading a devotional time in the evening. When John Langan, a Quaker from England, led it was my first time experiencing silence as a part of worship.

One weekend we all hitchhiked to St. Wolfgang. Tineka Nauta, Shirley Stauffer, John Langan and I decided to hike to the top of Schofsberg, a nearby mountain. We got on the wrong trail, had to retrace our steps, it got dark, the trail was steep and narrow and Shirley played out, she could not walk anymore. We managed to keep going slowly till we reached a meadow and a mountain home. We got permission to sleep in their barn. The next morning we hiked to the top, enjoyed the scenery a while, then took the cog train down and hitchhiked home. Another weekend several of us hiked up a mountain not far from Salzburg and stayed at a cabin near the top overnight. These weekends were an introduction to hiking for me and I realized I really enjoy hiking.

I took off one week from the six week work camp and hitch-hiked with a Dutch Mennonite girl to Mennonite World Conference in Karlsruhe, Germany. Lisa, the Dutch girl held a small Dutch flag and I held a small American flag. We were picked up by an empty Dutch moving van pulling a trailer with a large glass front and seating for a family which was great for us. We stopped at Ulm for the night then continued our ride to Karlsruhe.

At Conference I met David Herschberger, an Amish boy from Arkansas, now in Pax in Vienna, for the first time. I also met Nancy Fisher, an Amish girl from Gap, Pa, and some Beachy Amish including Elam Kauffman from Bird-in-Hand Pa and Jake Hershberger from Virginia. It seemed a bit awkward to speak in Pennsylvania Dutch after not having heard or spoken it for over two years. I had some difficulty staying awake through some of the Conference sessions as I was not used to sitting still that long. I enjoyed the Conference. It was especially great meeting so many people I knew. After Conference I rode with the Vienna Pax boys back to Salzburg and another week of Work Camp.

After the farewells and cleaning up at Work Camp I sent my large suitcase by freight to Kaiserslautern and hitchhiked alone to Munich, Germany. At Munich I got the train to Dauchau, one of the German Concentration camps where Jews were exterminated. It was not a pleasant experience. After Dauchau I hitchhiked to Kohlhof, the home of Christel Klassen who had been at Work Camp. I stayed with her a day then she took me on her motor scooter to Kaiserslautern. At Enkenbach by Kaiserslautern I met Amos Mast from Thomas, Oklahoma, another Amish boy in Pax. While in Kaiserslautern for two days I prepared for my 3 1/2 week trip to Scandanavia. Orpha Zimmerly helped me patch my raincoat. I bought a sleeping bag for the trip.

SCANDANAVIA - ESPELKAMP

On September 3, four of us, Arlin Hunsberger, I and two American boys but not Paxers, Alfred and Ted, left in the MCC VW Bug for the Scandanavian countries of Denmark, Sweden, Finland, and Norway. On our way the first day we had dinner with the Wedel Pax boys in North Germany: Glenn Kisamore, Wilson Myers, Dale Short, Albert Keim, John Kauffman, Forrest King, and Marlin Gerber. We then slept in a barn near Copenhagen. Throughout our trip we only slept in a motel four or five times. In Sweden we spent a weekend with Albert Joelson at Kumlo who had been in Work Camp. Albert's family was Baptist while the state church is Lutheran and we got to fellowship with the Baptist young people. We then visited Urban and June from near Uppsala who had also been at Work Camp. Urban gave us a tour of Stockholm.

From Sweden we took a boat across the Gulf of Bothnia to Finland. Sometime after Helsinki, Finland, we were at the Russian border and could see into Russia. This was rather thrilling for us as Russia was a closed Communist country at that time. In Lapland we were close to 100 miles above the Arctic circle and drove into Norway from Finland. We took route 50 south through Norway and eventually saw the beautiful fjords and drove down to the sea at one of them with many hairpin curves. We tried to locate Alfred Peterschmidt, a brother to Willy whom we knew, but were unsuccessful. We did visit Vigelan Park near Oslo with its many sculptures. Arrived back at Kaiserslautern September 27. We were gone 25 days, traveled 6,200 miles and it cost me $172.00 including everything, souvenirs, postage stamp, eating, etc. I thought it would be great to go to the fjords for my honeymoon, but I didn't.

Before leaving Kaiserslautern for Espelkamp where I would work for five weeks, I had coffee with John Kauffman and Albert Keim, now two good friends of mine. I also attended baptismal services at the new Enkenbach Mennonite Church. I sent my suitcase by freight to Espelkamp and I hitchhiked with a great deal of difficulty. When I arrived at Espelkamp everyone was in bed.

Espelkamp in northern Germany was a large munitions factory complex during World War II. It was so well camouflaged that it was never discovered and destroyed by the Allies. This was the site of the first Pax Unit of 20 American boys in 1951. When I arrived in 1957 it was no longer a Pax Unit. John Gingerich, a Conservative Mennonite from Ohio, had been there since 1949. Espelkamp was now under Conservative Mennonite Missions. However, two Pax boys, Kenneth Yoder from Grantsville, Md. and Harold Miller from Wellman, Iowa were assigned there and later joined by Glenn Kisamore from Hatfield, Pa. I was released from Pax after I left Work Camp and had completed my required two years of alternative military service. For the five weeks at Espelkamp I was sponsored by Amish Mennonite Aid. MCC needed $75.00 per month or $1,800.00 for two years support for each Pax boy. Most of the Mennonite boys received this support from their home church. I, as some others, had to pay my own way. But from that support we had all our expenses related to work paid for two years and we received a $10.00 per month allowance which was greatly appreciated. So after Espelkamp all my expenses were on my own except for my boat passage home over the Atlantic. My main work at Espelkamp was helping dismantle a bunker, save the lumber and bricks for re-use, digging out for a basement and digging a ditch for a drainage pipe. There was a small Mennonite Church here and we Pax boys participated in many of their activities.

Just before leaving Espelkamp I hitchhiked to Berlin. Had several rides to the border of East Germany, one on a motorcycle. At the border I waited till someone agreed to take me through East Germany to Berlin. With proper permission you could travel through East Germany on the Autobahn but you were not permitted to get off anywhere. In Berlin I stayed at Joe Roths who were in charge of Menno Heim. I visited a refugee camp that still had 3,500 refugees but at one time had over 8,000. I joined a bus tour of East Berlin and was shocked at how barren and empty it was. One of the interesting things in West Berlin was exhibits in the new modern Congresse Halle. Included in the large picture exhibition of the USA were some Lancaster County Amish. In a picture of the New Holland Sales Barn I recognized Isaac King our neighbor. After four days in Berlin I hitchhiked back to Espelkamp. On November 6 I said my good-byes there and tried to hitchhike to Kaiserslautern but took train and bus the last sixty miles.

BIENENBERG, GREECE AGAIN AND HOME

I felt fortunate that I was able to arrange to participate in the three month winter session of the European Mennonite Bible School in Switzerland before returning home. I was thrilled to have Dad and my oldest brother, Christian, join me for the last six weeks of Bible School. Bible School would be held in Bienenberg by Liestal, a new location at a former hotel on a hilltop. Formerly the school was held in Basel.

After leaving Espelkamp I spent two days at Kaiserslautern and Enkenbach. From there Wilson Myers from Doylestown, Pa. now in Pax two years, and I took the train to Basel, Switzerland.

From Basel we found our way to the beautiful former hotel on the hilltop, Bienenberg, where Bible School would be held. A third ex-Paxer, Marlin Gerber from Bluffton, Ohio was also taking three month Bible School. Classes were offered in either French or German. We Paxers of course took German which I found to be a bit difficult. I had to learn many new words and do all my assignments in German. Forty some students were enrolled, a few more German than French. My roommate was Herman Oesch from France who could speak German and French. We had excellent teachers. Adolf Schnebele, Samuel Gerber and Uncle, or Cornelius, Wall were my German teachers. Willy Peterschmidt, Glenn Good, an American, and Adolf Schnebele taught French classes. It took me several weeks to get used to writing in German. Besides taking classes we all needed to take our turn helping to prepare meals which often included peeling potatoes, washing dishes, cleaning, etc. It was an enjoyable time.

For Christmas vacation Wilson Myers and I were invited to stay with the Walter Geiser family near Tvennes in the Ura, the French speaking section of Switzerland. On Christmas Day we went to the nearby Catholic Church for a concert because two girls, Pieriete and Susette, that seemed like part of the Geiser family sang in the choir. Before Christmas Wilson and I had hiked up a mountain near the Geiser home with Pieriete and Susette. On the top we were above the clouds and could see the Alps above the clouds approximately 80 miles distant. I can still partially visualize that scene.

After Christmas Marlin Gerber, with his VW Bug, picked up Wilson and me and we drove through Interlaken and Bern back to Bienenberg. There we picked up our mail, met Isabelle Gingerich and set out for Alsace and Luxembourg to visit the homes of some Bible School friends. We visited Marie Claire Hirschy at Colmar, Werner Hirschler at Geisberg and the Philipp Hege family at Schaffsbusch. The Heges have 16 children. One of them, Erica, is married to Frank Shirk and lives in Leola, Pa. Twins, Theo and Martha Hege, were at Bible School. We also visited with Herman Oesch, my roommate, then went to Martha Oesch's home in Luxembourg.

From Oeschs in Luxembourg I got on a train to Paris and LaHavre, France, where Dad and Brother Christ were scheduled to arrive on the French ship Liberte. I arrived at LeHavre at 9:00, tried to get information about the arrival of Liberte but couldn't so I got a hotel room. The next afternoon, January 2 around 4:30 the ship Liberte pulled in and I got a glimpse of Brother Christ on the ship. At 5:30 I was allowed on board and met Dad and Brother Christ whom I had not seen or talked with for almost three years. We boarded a train to Paris, arriving at 10:05 and got a hotel room for 1,200 francs or about $3.00. From Paris we went to Martha Oesch's home in Luxembourg again and enjoyed visiting with the family. We met Noah Good and Horst Gerlach while there. For the weekend we went to Dudelange where Daniel and Betty (Gingerich) Troyer were serving in a Conservative Mennonite Mission. Noah Good was our Sunday School teacher and Horst Gerlach preached. We also met Omar Stahls and Glenn Goods and many Bible School students there. On Monday we boarded the train for Basel, Switzerland and from there a local train to Liestal. Because it was raining Herr Keller made several trips and brought all of us Bible School students from the Bahnhof to Bienenberg. With several new students there were now fifty-six of us. The first day of second semester Bible School, January 7, was Dad's seventy-third birthday but we did not inform any of the students.

We were fully involved with Bible School Monday through Friday but weekends were different. Sometimes we visited nearby Mennonite churches where Bible School students gave a program. One Sunday a program was given at Tvennes, an hour and a half drive, and Brother Christ, Dad and I had a nice visit with Walter Geisers where I had been for Christmas. Another weekend we were at Colmar in Alsace, France. Brother Christ, Dad, Marie Clair Hirschy and I went with Marlin Gerber in his VW. We drove through many vineyards, saw old and interesting dorfs or villages with walls around them, visited a torture chamber and drove through the town where Jacob Ammonn lived. Another Saturday Daniel Gerber, a student, Dad, Brother Christ and I went to Zurich and saw some things of Anabaptist interest concerning Zwingli, Felix Manz, Conrad Grebel, Blaurock, the Limmat River, etc. At Bible School Dad and Brother Christ seemed to fit in very well. And we decided that after Bible School we would take a two week trip to Greece where I lived and worked for two years. We would rent the MCC VW Bug and Waldemar Eger, a German boy and a student at Bienenberg would go along to help drive.

On February 9, the last Sunday eve of Bible School, Dad, Brother Christ and I each had a farewell speech. On Monday morning the students sang a farewell for us at the car and Uncle Wall had a prayer for us. The four of us then headed for Yugoslavia and Greece. We had beautiful scenery in the Alps. At Gotthard we needed to put our VW on a railroad car through the tunnel as the road over the mountain is closed in winter. We slept in Como, Italy our first night, spent several hours in Venice, the city with canals rather than streets, and were just north of Trieste, Italy by the Yugoslavia border our second night. Our drive through Yugoslavia was interesting for all of us, especially from Belgrade south. Very few motor vehicles but people walking, going to market, working in the fields. We stopped at a market and bought several things. Roads were mountainous.

We reached the Greek border at 7:00 pm and it took us two hours to get through both borders. It was 10:00 when we reached Salonica or Thessalonica and got a hotel room. Friday we visited the Quaker Farm School near Salonica then drove to Village

Tsakones where I met many of my old friends. Dad and Brother Christ slept at "Grandpa's". Harry Zimmerman made breakfast for us and walked with us to the cannery in Rothinia. Dad, Brother Christ and I walked through Rothinia and Tsakones and did a lot of visiting. Harry had lunch ready for us at the Pax Unit after which we drove to Aridea and a few neighboring villages. In the evening we had many visitors and I did not get to bed till 2:00 am. On Sunday morning we attended the Greek Church then Ann Ewert and Jack, our interpreter went with us to Sophie's home for the noon meal. In the afternoon we, that is Waldemar, Dad, Brother Christ and I, drove to Panayitsa where we saw the Brown Swiss cows. Brother Christ went with one of the Pax boys at 3:00 am to deliver milk in Edessa. Waldemar, Dad and I met them on the way back and we headed for Athens, stopping at Berea and spending time at Delphi. Delphi includes a well preserved 400 BC hillside stadium that could seat 6,500 spectators. Over the high mountain road on our way we were all impressed there were no guard rails.

At Athens we of course had a tour of Mars Hill and the Acropolis but we also visited Roy Umbles from Goshen, Ind. Roy is teaching at Pierce College. After Athens we spent half a day at Corinth then headed for Ionnina We missed the last ferry of the day across the Corinthian Gulf so we slept near Patra.. In the morning there was a long line of vehicles waiting to cross the ferry because the king and queen of Greece were coming across the ferry and everyone had to wait. We saw the royalty vehicle and entourage go by us. We spent a little time at the Brethren Church Unit at Ionnina then drove, at times above the clouds, to the coast and got a ferry to the Island of Corfu. At 5:00 in the evening we boarded a ship for Brindisi, Italy, deck class meaning we had to sleep on deck. Dad and Waldemar slept on benches and were uncomfortably cold. We arrived at Brindisi at 4:30 a.m. but it took us three hours to get through customs.

Leaving the Adriatic Sea at Brindisi we drove west across Italy over some crooked and mountainous roads reaching Pompei then Naples along the Tyrrhenian Sea where we slept. Interesting along the way were the olive groves, big wheeled carts, towns built on mountain peaks and walled in. In the morning when we went to leave Naples we discovered our VW had been broken into. Nearly all our extra clothes were taken, about $75.00 worth. We drove on to Rome where we got rooms in a hotel near St. Peter's Church for $1.60 each. We spent several hours in Rome yet on Monday forenoon then drove along the sea at times but also over mountains, saw the Leaning Tower of Pisa and slept near Genoa, right on the waterfront. Now headed for Bienenberg we again put our vehicle on a railroad car to go through the tunnel at Gotthard, drove through Altdorf, famous for William Tell, Luzern and Rigi Kulm arriving back at Bienenberg at 6:00.

Dad and Brother Christ had now experienced Bible School and visiting Greece but had not yet been to Germany so we headed north. We drove through the Schwartzwald to Waldemar's home near Enkenbach, were introduced to his parents, had lunch there and said, "Auf Wiedersehen", to Waldemar. Waldemar had been with us on our trip to Greece. At Enkenbach I showed Dad and Brother Christ where I had worked for six months and introduced them to many people. On our way north to Espelkamp we stopped at Brethren Service Headquarters in Kassel and had a nice time there with "Kaffee and Kuchen" as they explained Heifer Project to us and where the heifers were placed. Had supper and overnight at Espelkamp where John and Grace Gingerich are in charge and we also met Kenneth Yoder, Harold Miller and Glenn Kisamore, the Pax boys.

Then we headed for Berlin. The roads were snowy and icy ever since we left Enkenbach. On the Autobahn to the East German border we slid off the road twice, once giving us a flat tire. It scared us considerably and I drove slower. At the East German border we got permission to drive the seventy-five miles through East Germany on the only road open to Berlin and all exits were closed. In Berlin we stayed at Joe Roths who are in charge of Menno Heim. Among other things I took Dad and Brother Christ to Congresse Halle and showed them the exhibit of Lancaster County including New Holland Sales Barn.

On our way back to Frankfurt we stopped at Cochem, near Koblentz, and visited the Wally Schorat family that had received one of Brother Christ's heifers two years ago through Heifer Project. We had stopped and toured the Cologne Cathedral on our way. At Frankfurt we met Peter Dyck, Orpha Zimmerly and others we knew. We turned in our VW to MCC and settled for it with John Hostetler. We had put on 8,089 kilometer, approximately 4,853 miles. It cost us about 6 ½ cents a mile, for the car. Now we head for Liverpool, England and home.

Dad, Brother Christ and I got on a local train at Frankfurt and soon after midnight got on the Balkan Express at Mainz and came to Ostende, Belgium. There were Greeks on the train and I enjoyed speaking Greek again. At Ostende we went through customs, had a two hour boat ride across the English Channel to Dover then a train to London. Had a free afternoon in London then at 9:05 Friday morning got on a special Cunard Line train to Liverpool where we had tickets for the ship RMS Sylvania.

Leaving London we enjoyed going through some very nice farmland, lots of pasture, some sheep and individual farm buildings rather than farm villages. The train went through Birmingham, Stafford and Crewe arriving at Liverpool soon after noon. A special bus took us to our boat. We boarded and were scheduled to leave at 3:00 pm on Saturday, March 8 but because of high winds did not leave until midnight. We stopped at Cork, the southern tip of Ireland, picked up 120 passengers, lots of luggage and freight and headed for the Atlantic.

Dad, Brother Christ and I had a room to ourselves with four beds and running water. Our first day out was Sunday and we attended a non-denominational service held in the lounge. Everyone had assigned tables around which to eat. We had a table for six with three English women. On our six day journey we relaxed, had devotions together every morning in our room, read, visited with other passengers, played games including ping pong and table tennis and watched the never ending waves in the ocean. We traveled around 500 miles a day without much change of scenery. Before arriving at New York we stopped at Halifax, Nova Scotia. Brother Christ and I walked through town for about an hour. It seemed good to get back on American soil but I almost felt sorry that from now on everyone would speak English, no more German, Greek, Dutch, French, Spanish, etc. It was snowing and blowing as we approached New York, very rough. It was snowing or raining as we docked at 6:00 pm. We got off at 7:00, waited for our luggage till 8:00 and no one was there to meet us so we got bus tickets for Gap. Just as we were leaving for the bus depot Jonas Stoltzfus, Alvin Lapp, Benuel Glick, Mervin King, Ben Stoltzfus, Frieda Stoltzfus, Naomi Lantz, Mary Ann Riehl, Anna Mary Lapp, Mary Fisher and Sarah Fisher walked by. We redeemed our tickets and came home with them. Now at home in Buena Vista we had ice cream together. And so ended my three years of Pax.

CHAPTER 7

College

Returning from my three years in Europe my home was with my parents in a house at the crossroad in Buena Vista. My first full day home, Saturday, March 15,1958 my brothers and sisters living nearby came to visit: Christian married to Naomi Beiler, Seth married to Hazel Burkholder, Sylvia married to John U. Lapp and Lena married to Ben B. Beiler Jr. We had oyster soup and ice cream for dinner, our noon meal. My sister Elizabeth married to Harvey E. Miller from Nappanee, Indiana and my brother John married to Floy Zook from Port Allengany, Pa. soon came to visit also. The second day home, Sunday, I went to church with Dad at Steff's Elams. Buck Sam Stoltzfus and Levi Fisher preached. The message was much the same as I had remembered it from three years earlier.

On Monday I went to Brother Seth to work on his dairy farm near Nottingham for a week. On Wednesday it began to snow and rain and continued for 24 hours, mostly snow. It left two feet of heavy snow on the ground. Almost all electric and telephone wires were down as well as numerous tree branches and some buildings. At Seth's we had no telephone or electric for seven days. We had to milk over 20 cows by hand and make a path for the cows to get water from a spring in the meadow. After several days Seth and I loaded 21 cans of milk on the manure spreader and with the tractor pulling the spreader, I went through the fields and partially opened roads to the milk plant several miles away. The plant was closed because of no electric but we dumped the milk into a tank truck and it was taken to Philadelphia for pasteurizing.

For the summer I got a job with John Dienner, an Amish carpenter contractor. Much of our work was rebuilding or repairing sheds, porches and small buildings that collapsed during the snow in March. Brother Christ's son Alvin had my horse and buggy while I was in Europe and now he returned them as Alvin got a car. I now had my own transportation. I participated in "Group" activities such as socials, Bible studies and singing regularly at the Kanagy Old People's Home. I also participated some with the Beachy Amish youth activities. A few of us ex-Paxers, LaMar and Bob Stauffer, Arlin Hunsberger, Marvin Moyer, Lester Yoder and I, attended the Greek Easter Service in Lancaster on South Queen Street. The big celebration is right after midnight.

While still in Europe I decided I would probably go to college in the fall and prepare to be a teacher. It was rather difficult to inform my parents that this is what I wanted to do. But I did tell them and they were not happy about my decision. But like my going to Pax they eventually accepted it. I was hoping I could go without being excommunicated from Church so I went to see our bishop, Buck Sam Stoltzfus. I explained I wanted to be a teacher. He made no promises but I felt assured I would not be excommunicated just for going to college. I had been out of school 14 years and no high school so I was required to take tests to see if Eastern Mennonite College would accept me. I made arrangements to take the tests under supervision of Mennonite Pastor Abner Stoltzfus at his home. I passed and was accepted.

On September 3 ex-Paxer John Kauffman came to our house, I said good-bye to Mom and Dad and we drove to Eastern Mennonite College, EMC, in Harrisonburg, Va. We picked up John Shearer in Elizabethtown on the way. I knew I would be somewhat of a misfit, Amish and 28 years old when the majority of freshmen were just out of high school and 17 or 18 years old. Not having been to high school I did not know how classes were organized, how to read the college catalog, etc. A big help to my adjustment was that there were nine other ex-Paxers there, eight of them freshmen and I knew all of them. Bob Weaver, Marvin Moyer, Wilson Myers, Ben Yoder, Albert Keim, Luke Martin, Carl Beyeler and Ira Zook. I decided to take German 1, taught by Ernest Gehman as one of my classes. I wanted to understand German grammar and I thought maybe I would teach German sometime. Also I figured I might need a class not so difficult to counter the potential difficult ones. Our first weekend on campus we freshmen all camped out in the mountains, boys and girls separately. Elam Stauffer and Andrew Leatherman got lost in the evening and did not get back to camp until the next day. Throughout the year I made friends with the international students from Ethiopia, Uganda, Japan, Germany, and Vietnam and spent considerable time with them.

During the year I made several trips home from EMC for Council Meeting, Communion, and Christmas. But one unplanned trip home was for the funeral of my brother-in-law Ben B. Beiler Jr. He had not been well for several months, went to Florida thinking it might help but didn't. He died in the Ephrata Hospital near home during surgery. Cancer was discovered. Ben died November 19, 1958 at age 40. He and Lena had seven children, six boys and one girl. Paul, the youngest, was nine months old when his father died and his mother became a widow.

At EMC I needed to work rather hard to fulfill my assignments, prepare for tests, etc. However I always took Sunday off and did no school work on Sunday. Weekends I often went with several others to a mission church at Elkton east of Harrisonburg. Several non-routine weekends that I especially enjoyed were one that about a dozen of us hiked Massanutten Peak. Another weekend nine of us, mostly ex-Paxers, went home with Albert Keim and slept out on the Blue Ridge Mountain one of the nights. Overall I enjoyed my freshman year of college. I had my last test on Friday May 29 and at 5:30 I left for Lancaster County with Luke Martin. Albert Keim came along.

Following are some weddings I attended spring and summer of 1959:

May 23: Bob Stauffer and Evelyn Buckwalter
May 30: Reuben Stoltzfus and Anna Mary Lapp. Anna
    Mary is my niece, Brother Christ's daughter
June 7: Paul Miller and Martha Yoder at Goshen, Indiana
June 13: Arlin Hunsberger and Naomi Derstine. I was
    best man for Arlin.

At home for the summer other than attending weddings I worked for John Dienner as a carpenter and for my brother Seth on his farm as well as a few days for my brother John on his farm in McKeen County. I spent some weekends with Arno Thimm from Germany who was an MCC Trainee with the Ben Hershey family at Spring Garden only a few miles from us.

My sophomore year at EMC was rather uneventful and I enjoyed it. I remember the course "How We Got Our Bible" by G. Irvin Lehman was troubling for me. How can we use the Bible to help us understand God and God's will has remained a challenge for me much of my life. I joined a group of 29 students for a three day tour of Washington DC with D. Ralph Hostetter that was educational and interesting. 1960 was leap year and I'm still amazed that Rita Halteman asked me, an Amish student, for a date! Rita became well known as an editor, author and professor with a Ph.D. and I'm still impressed that she asked me for a date. When I decided to go to college I thought I might just go two years so I enrolled in Junior College. Thus I graduated from Junior College in 1960. My sister-in-law Hazel Lapp and her two children Donna Belle and James came for my graduation as did Mary Ann Riehl. Mary Ann later received her BS and sufficient additional education to teach a nursing school until retirement age. She remained a member of the Amish Church.

After graduation I hitchhiked from Harrisonburg, Va., to Chambersburg, Pa. then got a Greyhound home. At home I again worked for John Dienner as a carpenter. On July 9 I attended the wedding of LaMar Stauffer and Kathryn Mann at Lancaster Mennonite High School. And for the 1960-61 school year I taught upper grades at Linville Hill Mennonite School.

My parents were quite unhappy when I informed them I would be going to EMC again in the fall rather than teach another year. If I had not already made arrangements with Linville Hill Mennonite School and Eastern Mennonite College, I might have decided to continue teaching rather than go back to college. Now I could hardly change plans anymore. And I would attend Summer School at EMC then the full 1961-62 term. I took the Greyhound for 10 weeks of Summer School at EMC.

1961-62 was my last full year at EMC but because I did not have enough credits to be a senior at the beginning of the year I did not graduate with my class. I graduated after summer school in 1963. I did enjoy my last full year at EMC. Astronomy 101 taught by John Horst was the most mind-expanding course I took all through college. It was my first real introduction to the solar system, space, galaxies, etc. It was almost unbelievable but I believed it.

I was informed a blind student, Daniel Bowman, was enrolled and on campus. I kept looking for him but could not pick him out, he just blended in with everyone else. Eventually though I got to know him and he became a friend. He later married my cousin Ferne Lapp, and became accomplished as a piano tuner, marble frame builder and a documentary DVD was made about him. He and Ferne raised three daughters.

After Easter vacation I had the opportunity to accompany the International Students from EMC to a Foreign Student Conference at Hesston College in Kansas. There were two car loads and I was asked to drive the one car. Professor Homer Mumaw and his wife drove the other car. Twenty-eight countries were represented at the conference and I found it interesting and challenging. We had an unfortunate experience in Missouri when we stopped at a restaurant. Because of African Americans with us we were refused service. We could not eat in Missouri which was sad and embarrassing. I was an elementary education major and did my student teaching at Singers Glen.

The summer of 1962 I took some courses at Millersville State College near Lancaster. The school year 1963-64 I again taught at Linville Hill Mennonite School. After finishing the school year at Linville Hill I went to five weeks of summer school at EMC and graduated in absentia with a BS in Education. That ended my college days except for taking several courses at Millersville State College and Elizabethtown College during the summers while I was teaching. But best of all I married right after finishing EMC.

CHAPTER 8

Marriage and Family

When I was 18 or 19 I went steady with a girl for about six weeks, steady meaning we agreed to date each other and no one else. After six weeks she wanted to break the commitment so we did. Sometime after I returned from Europe I corresponded with a girl from Indiana for some months and we were together several times but we mutually agreed to discontinue our special relationship. During much of 1961 I dated a fine local Amish girl with many talents. However the relationship just didn't seem quite right to me and after sharing this with her we discontinued our special relationship. My parents and her mother, a widow, had assumed we would marry and were quite disappointed and unhappy that we discontinued our special relationship.

Soon after breaking up this special relationship I began to take more notice of Sara Ellen Miller, an Amish girl on campus at EMC from Holmes County, Ohio. We knew each other and at times went to Elkton to church together. I decided to ask her to go with me to nearby Lindale Mennonite Church to hear Don Augsburger preach on a Sunday eve and she said she would. Before parting I asked if she would go with me to hear "The Messiah" being given at nearby Bridgewater College in about two weeks and again she consented. I was impressed at how much we seemed to enjoy being together. We had several more dates and when Sara Ellen completed her college at mid-semester and went home we decided to write to each other. Sara came back to campus to graduate with the 1962 class with a BS in Education. After taking five weeks of summer school I went to Ohio to see her and was introduced to her parents and her brothers and sisters. And I asked her the age old universal question, "Will you?" She said, "Yes, I will."

The year following our engagement I taught upper grades at Linville Hill Mennonite School near my home and Sara Ellen taught first and second grade at Beidler School in Holmes County Ohio. We wrote letters to each other about every week and planned our wedding for July 27, 1963 at her home. The wedding ceremony where we said our vows to each other was at the nearby Ivan Miller farm in their new implement shed. After the nearly four hour ceremony we went with horse and buggy from Ivans to Sara Ellen's home where we had the noon meal and we opened our gifts. Fred's Christ Stoltzfus and Benuel Glick with Betty Burkholder and Alma Keim were our attendants. We were honored to have an International Student, Thompson Sabiti from Uganda, at our wedding and a work camp friend John Langan from England. For our honeymoon Sara Ellen and I had a cabin rented for a week at Pymatuning State Park in Northeastern Ohio. After our honeymoon we rented a truck to bring Sara's belongings to Lancaster County. Sara left her home in Holmes County and came to live with me in a home we rented in Buena Vista by Gap, Pa.

Our first home was in the "Daudy end" of Samuel and Katie Beiler's large farm house. It was just across a small field from where my parents lived since 1955. Sara needed to adjust to the Amish church and community in Lancaster County which was some different from Holmes County and I had to adjust as a married man in the church which included raising a beard. And Sara and I had to learn how to live with each other and enjoy each other. Sara got whooping cough rather seriously in the fall which made it unpleasant for her and she was pregnant. But a great event took place July 16, the birth of our first child, Nathan James. It was a deep spiritual experience for both of us to hold our firstborn and dedicate him to God. Our church, neighbors and friends celebrated with us. The second Sunday Sara and Nathan were home from the hospital we had 33 church people, neighbors, and friends stop by to congratulate us and celebrate with us.

In the summer of 1964 I helped Dad and a few carpenters build an addition to Mother and Dad's house. In the fall of 1964 Sara, Nathan and I moved into the new addition. Mother and Dad lived in the "daudy end". We had an agreement that Mother and Dad would always speak Pa Dutch to Nathan and Sara and I would speak English. This worked quite well and Nathan learned both languages. He would always speak Pa Dutch to the Amish and English to the non-Amish. On occasion we would ask Nathan to tell Grandpa and Grandma something then Sara and I would sneak and listen to what he told them. He would always tell them in Pa Dutch what we told him in English.

In the summer of 1965 Sara and I decided to leave the Amish Church and join Sandy Hill Mennonite Church. Before we married we had agreed that we would eventually need to make this change for two reasons, we did not want our children to go through "Rumspringa" in their teen years and we could not conscientiously keep the "meidung" or shunning as required by the church. And transportation was a problem. Teaching at Linville Hill Mennonite School did not provide the finances we needed to raise a family and having a car would make it so much easier to get another job. We informed my parents of our decision. They were of course sad but not really surprised. And in a sense we received their blessing. They wished though we would join the Beachy Amish who had cars rather than the Mennonites but we didn't. After our change it was difficult to meet my Amish relatives, neighbors and friends and acknowledge we were leaving the Amish church. We of course were excommunicated from the church and put in the ban. But we just felt we needed to do this. We continue to have high respect and love for all our Amish friends and neighbors. They are also God's people and have a great culture and community.

I should add here that a year or so after we left the Old Order Amish the New Order Amish church began. Mother and Dad were part of that and it was a very good home church for them. They no longer needed to shun us. We could now eat at the same table and they could drive with us. "God is good."

Sara and I were blessed with three more children, Michael Omar born June 6, 1966 (6-6-66), Irene Elizabeth born October 18,1967 and Herman David born June 14, 1971. We considered each of them a gift from God and they have all been a real blessing to us. Family life however was not as ideal as I had envisioned it would be. Sara and I had some communication problems and our children were not always well behaved and respectful. Probably the best decision we ever made in our married life was to attend a Marriage Encounter Weekend in Denver, Pa. in the fall of 1983. We were greatly blessed and our life was changed. It effected the way we related to our children as well as to each other. Sara and I became presenters for Marriage Encounter and were involved with Marriage Encounter Weekends for over 20 years.

After teaching for seven years I switched jobs and worked at Provident Bookstore in Lancaster for 30 years. While the children were in elementary school we lived mostly on my income. Sara had occasional jobs as substitute teaching and working for IU13 helping Old Order Mennonite children adjust to first grade in public school. Her additional income helped but we were limited financially. Also for a period of time Sara was cashier at Rhoads Store, a popular grocery store in Buena Vista. The store was established in 1850 and was in business over 150 years. Local Amish grocery stores eventually took its place. At one time Lapp Post Office was located in Rhoads Store.

We were fortunate the year Herman was born we found out about cabins available to rent for a week in certain Pennsylvania State Parks that we could afford. So in 1972 we rented a cabin in Clear Creek State Park in Jefferson County for a week for $32.00. We had a wonderful weeks vacation and continued doing this the next twelve or more years in about every Pennsylvania State Park that had cabins to rent. Later Sara got an almost full time job at Provident Bookstore which helped us financially. Overall we had an enjoyable family life. For a brief time we had four teenagers, three boys and a girl, and they were lots of fun. To keep our meal-times somewhat orderly we had two strict rules, two burps and you do the dishes, one fart and you do the dishes. Otherwise we did a "horse and goggle" which I learned in Pax to see who does the dishes. It worked rather well.

My dad died September 1975 at age 90. His funeral was in the barn on the farm he lived for 20 years, from 1935-1955. He was buried in the Spring Garden cemetery where his parents and grandparents are buried. Dad had asked Bishop John Mast from Kansas to preach at his funeral so John had the main sermon. At the time of the funeral my three sisters were widows. Now Mother was a widow also. Mother died two years later in October 1977 at age 89. Because she was bedfast she was with Sister Sylvia most of the last year of her life and the funeral was at Sylvia's and her son Mose. Mother of course is also buried in the Spring Garden cemetery.

With both Mother and Dad gone our family of six now had the whole house. Because of being built at three different times it did not fit together too well. The original stone house was built in the 1890s, an addition built around 1910 and our end in 1964. For the next 30 years after Mother and Dad died, we made good use of our large house hosting our children's friends and many small groups from the church. Our children eventually all married and moved out. In 2006 Sara and I moved out also into a double wide trailer just a few yards away. Nathan, our oldest son bought the property and moved in with his wife and six children.

At Mother's funeral we children, that is my brothers, sisters and I were aware there was no longer a central place to meet and we agreed to plan an annual Mose and Rachel Lapp reunion. The seven children would take turns hosting the reunions. Because Philip Beiler was getting married in Indiana in June of 1978 it was decided Lizzie would host the first reunion at her home in Indiana at that time. It would then begin with Christian the oldest and continue by age. So from 1978 to 2005 we had 27 reunions usually with 50-100 people. Often someone was assigned to give a report on an ancestor or a family member, we had "freundschaft" quizzes and lots of fun games especially for children. I was in charge to see that the reunions happened. Eventually each family was large enough to have their own reunions and the Mose and Rachel Lapp reunions were discontinued. Our last reunion was hosted by John and Floy at their son Davids in Lowville, NY. And so ends my chapter of Marriage and Family. I am now the only one of my siblings still living. My younger brother John died unexpectedly two years ago.

Buena Vista School where I attended.

The children at Linville Hill Mennonite School with me their teacher.

Me with my horse.

Engaged couple, Sara and Omar.

Our wedding day, Omar and Sara

My EMC graduation picture   *Sara, Omar, and Nathan by our house.*

Sara, Omar, Sister Lena, Brother John and Floy

Sister Lena, Brother Seth, Brother John, Me

50th Wedding Anniversary: Sara and Omar, 2013

Sara, Omar and four children: Irene, Nathan, Michael, Herman

Sara, Omar, Irene, Sherilyn, Nathan, Herman, Farrah, Karen, Michael

Eight of our nine grandchildren plus a spouse holding a great-grandson.

Our home in Buena Vista. Sara and I now live in the double wide trailer on the picture.

CHAPTER 9

School Teacher

For my first year of teaching I left home in Buena Vista every Monday morning and drove to Elvin and Ruth Beilers approximately two miles west of Gap along Mine Road, about six miles from home, with my horse and buggy. Elvins had board and lodging for my horse and me five days a week. From Elvins I had a 10 or 15 minute walk to Linville Hill School. I think I had 28 students. I taught grades 5-8 mostly Old Order and Beachy Amish with a few Mennonite children. It was a two-room school and grades 1-4 were in an adjoining room. It was a rather difficult year for me partly because of a few older boys with whom I did not communicate very well. I spent evenings at Elvins where I boarded preparing lessons and grading papers which I somewhat enjoyed. And some days at school were very good. However I sensed my need for more preparation and decided to return to college and get my degree in education.

After another year of college and summer school I had my second year of teaching at Linville Hill. I again boarded at Elvin and Ruth Beilers and it was very similar to my first year. Overall it was a good year but I again had some discipline problems and was very busy with lesson preparations and correcting papers. An extra inspiration for me was the weekly correspondence with Sara Ellen Miller. At the end of my second year of teaching I took five weeks of summer school at EMC and graduated with a four year degree. Then I went to Ohio and Sara Ellen and I were married.

Thus my next two years at Linville Hill were a bit different. Sara Ellen and I lived in Buena Vista and the Linville Hill School Board agreed to provide transportation for me. Three board members, Aaron Beiler, Ben Lapp, and Jake Miller took weekly turns to pick me up and bring me home. Ninth grade was added at Linville Hill and I needed to provide much of the curriculum which kept me busy. Somehow I sensed I was an okay teacher but not a really good teacher. The salary at Linville Hill was not the best so Sara Ellen and I decided to make a change.

The big change after four years at Linville Hill was we changed our church membership and got a car. I then taught certain subjects at Conestoga Christian School in Morgantown, Pa. I taught English Composition, Literature, Math, Algebra, Spelling, and German. Before teaching algebra I took an algebra course during the summer at Elizabethtown College as I had very little algebra background. My favorite teaching subject was German but algebra was probably my second favorite.

I especially enjoyed working with Pastor William Weaver, a fellow teacher at Conestoga who taught Bible and music. He had an excellent relationship with the students and I learned much from him. I also enjoyed working with Ed Kurtz the Principal and Paul Beiler and learned from them. I mostly enjoyed my three years at Conestoga Christian School. However we had three children and while teacher salary at Conestoga was considerably more than Linville Hill it did not meet our needs. I could double our income by teaching in a public school. If I remember correctly my first year of teaching I got $900.00 for the year, $100.00 per month. So I checked into teaching at Pequea Valley Elementary. But Sara Ellen said, "why don't you check into other job possibilities. You don't have to be a teacher all your life." I checked other possibilities and made a major decision. I would not continue in my teaching career.

CHAPTER 10

Provident Bookstore

In the spring of 1968 I checked into job possibilities at three places, Pequea Valley Elementary School, Weavers Poultry at New Holland and Provident Bookstore in Lancaster. Provident was the first to respond with a job offer and I decided to take it even though the other two would have been better pay. Aaron Hollinger was Personnel Manager, Charles Shenk General Manager and Lester Weber Book Department Supervisor when I was hired. My job was sales clerk in the book department and Lester Weber was my boss. It was a challenge to know the location of thousands of books and Bibles, help customers find them, learn how to take special orders and help keep books in stock. However I enjoyed it very much, it was easier than being a teacher and I had no homework and better pay. Wow! But it only lasted about a year when Lester decided to leave Provident and I was offered his job of being buyer and supervisor. I knew nothing about either and it scared me but I decided to take the offer. I had learned a lot about books and theology from Lester, especially theology. I had no theology course in college and Lester helped me at least partially understand the theology field for which I was grateful.

Now I had an office off the main floor and was responsible for purchasing all books and Bibles and keep a proper inventory. We had a stock card for every title which helped in reordering back-stock and I met with sales reps to purchase new titles. Elizabeth Frank was my first secretary and she helped me considerably.

Christian Booksellers Association, CBA, was big at that time and sponsored an annual convention every summer where hundreds of publishers presented their new titles and offered many specials. My first convention was in Denver, Colorado. I flew out from Cleveland, Ohio. Sara and our four children stayed at Sara's home in Holmes County, Ohio the week I was in Denver. Needless to say the CBA Convention was overwhelming for me and I didn't really know what I was doing. But I survived, the bookstore survived and I learned to enjoy my work. CBA Convention became an annual event for me and many times I was able to take Sara with me. Sometimes I took vacation before and after convention, Sara, the four children and I drove and we all enjoyed the week at the convention. Over the years Sara was along at Dallas, Anaheim, Denver, Cincinnati, St. Louis, Orlando, Minneapolis, Atlantic City and possibly other places.

I enjoyed providing book tables for local church events and conferences as well as helping at national church assemblies in various states even though they were a lot of work. I also helped with a book table at Mennonite World Conference in Winnipeg, Manitoba in 1990.

Even though I did not help produce it I was very proud of Provident Bookfinder, an excellent review of books issued four times a year. And I usually felt good about our spring and fall book promotions. I enjoyed working with Ron Meyer and Dorothy Cutrell from Mennonite Publishing House, Rose Hostetler from Scottdale Provident, Bertha Beachy from Goshen Provident, Becky Felton from Souderton Provident and others in deciding what books to promote.

A constant challenge of course was to keep inventory under control and have a profitable turnover. And for me the change to computers over the years was very frustrating and I was not always supportive. The first few years I was at Provident we would tell customers it would take 3-5 weeks for their special order to arrive and it usually did, sometimes longer. The last few years we could often tell them we could have it next day and we did.

When I started in 1968 book inventory was mostly controlled with a stock card for every title with all the sales information on the card. And I thought it worked pretty well. However 20 years later every title with all its sales history was available on a computer screen. If a customer asked for a certain title the computer screen would inform us how many we had and where it was located in the store. If we had none in stock the computer had information of how many copies our distributors had and if we could have it the next day. Ken Reinford from Souderton Provident, who became General Manager in 1988, was largely responsible to have this happen.

When I started at Provident, Lancaster had two branch stores, one in New Holland- the original Weavers Bookstore- and one in Ephrata. When Park City Mall opened in 1971 we opened our third branch store. All new items were purchased by buyers at the Lancaster store but branch stores reordered stock. Sometime after Ken Reinford became General Manager the buyers at Lancaster bought new items for Souderton and Doylestown stores also. I found it quite a challenge to keep customers and employees happy with my choice of books I put on the shelves. And I wasn't always sure myself. I represented a broad spectrum of theology and got considerable criticism for it from our theologically conservative customers. I spent much time in prayer about these criticisms.

I worked under four General Managers, Charles Shenk, John Shertzer, Richard Crockett and Ken Reinford. When Richard Crockett resigned in 1987 Ben Cutrell was interim manager for several months. I had quite a few different secretaries during my 25 years as buyer/ supervisor and they were all capable and more efficient with typewriters and computers than I was and did a great job. Next to getting computers our biggest change was moving from 40 East King Street in downtown Lancaster, the old Sears Roebuck building, to Lancaster Shopping Center, 1625 Lititz Pike, in 1987. I was sorry to leave Downtown Lancaster and wished we would stay but it was a profitable move and a wise choice. I retired from Provident in my 27th year on March 30, 1995. However five years later I got an excellent retirement job there in receiving under the supervision of Gary Herr for about nine years. During the time I was working in receiving in November 2006, Mennonite Publishing House sold all Provident Bookstores to Berea who already owned many bookstores mostly in the West. Nathan Humbert then became manager of the stores in Pennsylvania that had been Provident. I worked in receiving for Berea under the supervision of Gary Herr till almost the end of December 2008 after which they had no more work for me.

Provident Bookstores was a good place for me as I could handle middle management fairly well but could not have handled top management. I was aware there were people that knew books better than I and could have done a better job than I. But they were not willing to work for the salary buyer/supervisors got at Provident so it was the right career for me and I thanked God many times for my job. I was grateful for Mennonite Publishing House and Provident Bookstores. Praise the Lord!

CHAPTER 11

Marriage Encounter

Sara and I are both in our eighties, we enjoy being together, eating together, shopping together, sleeping together and helping each other. Life is good! In the summer of 1983 after 20 years of marriage we had a life-changing experience when we participated in a Marriage Encounter Weekend in Denver, Pa. It still affects us today. While we had a "good" marriage our first 20 years but it was not as good as I had anticipated. In my priorities I think marriage and family was number three, church was first, work second then marriage and family. I accepted the occasional arguments Sara and I had and the times we could not communicate as normal, not as ideal as I had dreamt but just the way it was and probably always would be. Then came our Marriage Encounter Weekend and we had an experience way beyond our expectations. God touched us and helped us communicate.

We participated in our first Marriage Encounter Weekend because of the invitation of Nevin Horst, a co-worker at Provident Bookstore and a friend. He asked me about our marriage and I said something about it being okay. He said it can be better than that. You should come to a Marriage Encounter Weekend. Because I had high respect for Nevin I thought maybe we should but didn't really expect it to help us much. Then Sara did not want to go. She did not want to share with other couples. Nevin assured us we would not need to share with others. So Sara rather reluctantly agreed and we went.

In the opening session it was obvious it would be a different and unusual weekend. We were informed there would be silence as we moved from session to session. And no introductions except our names. We would not ask people where they lived or their occupation and they would not ask us. We took off our watches, gave them to our spouse and said our time was theirs. We had no access to time over the weekend unless we cheated. That was all in the first hour and surprises kept coming all weekend. If you ever attended a weekend you know what some of them were.

The weekend began Friday evening and consisted basically of a group meeting in a conference room with everyone present. There two of the four presenting couples would sit on an elevated platform and share about their life. When finished everyone was dismissed and in silence each couple went to their room with an assignment. Our first assignment was to write a brief answer to, "Why did I come here this weekend?" and "What do I hope to gain?" then exchange our answers and discuss them. A bell left us know when to return to the conference room. At meal time there were questions for discussion on our table but no introductions. We all wore name tags. Sometime on Saturday we were informed that each couple present had a prayer couple who had previously taken a Marriage Encounter Weekend praying for us all weekend. By the end of the weekend Sara and I had discussed areas of our life we had never discussed before and also shared in a depth we had not previously. The weekend was life changing for us, a blessing beyond our expectations. The four presenting couples for our weekend were:Pastor couple Blanche and Nevin Horst, Marian and Henry Leaman, Martha and David Clymer, and Sue and Earl Showalter.

We were aware of course that the closeness we experienced would probably not last unless we made some changes. So we decided that five days a week we would get up a half hour earlier and have a 10/10, write a ten minute note to each other on an agreed subject, exchange notes and talk about them. We did this for many years. Several weeks after our weekend Henry and Marian Leaman asked us to be a presenting couple for Marriage Encounter. We knew how much we had been blessed so after several weeks of prayer we said yes. To be a presenting couple we had to follow an outline and write three presentations of our life experience. It was hard work and our "talks" were workshopped heavily. To be a presenting couple it was also required to take a "deeper five day encounter" given only by the Catholic Church. Sara and I went to Newark, NJ in March of 1984 and experienced that.

So in early fall of 1984 we were the rookie presenting couple at Denver, Pa, a year after our original Marriage Encounter there. Because we had all our presentations written we were fairly relaxed and the weekend went well. Within a year Sara and I wrote the presentations for the second presenting couple so we could give either set one or set two presentations, whichever was needed. We were a presenting couple for the next 16 years giving three or four weekends per year. The outlines were revised several times and we needed to rewrite everything at least twice. After no longer being a presenting couple Sara was a prayer partner coordinator for a number of years.

Four or five weekends a year were given at Kenbrook Bible Camp, a Brethren in Christ Center north of Lebanon, Pa. For many years at least one a year, sometimes two, were given at Black Rock Retreat near Kirkwood, Pa., Bird-in-Hand Motel and Restaurant in Bird in Hand, Pa., Best Western Country Cupboard , Lewisburg, Pa., a motel and restaurant in Williamsport, Pa.., a number of times at Penn York, Pa., Laurelville Mennonite Camp in Laurelville, Pa., and Beaver Camp near Lowville, NY. Sara and I were also at China Lake, Maine. Dwight and Edna Hershberger participated there and Dwight took us in a plane. Other distant places Sara and I helped give weekends were LaJunta, Colorado; Richmond, Virginia; Chesapeake, Virginia; and Montgomery, Alabama. Many many prayers covered every weekend. Sara and I had not presented many weekends until we always felt assured before we left home that God would anoint us and the weekend in a special way. Several weekends were given in Spanish in Central America and Mexico led by Bill and Judy Houser.

Mennonite and Brethren Marriage Encounter is part of Worldwide Marriage Encounter. Worldwide Marriage Encounter started in Spain in 1952 when a young priest, Father Gabriel Calvo, began developing a series of conferences for married couples. In 1967 Marriage Encounter Weekends were brought to America. They grew and became popular with many non-Catholic attending the weekends. Eventually the Catholic Church cooperated in making Marriage Encounter available to Protestant denominations. But to be called Marriage Encounter the Catholic outlines had to be followed. Each denomination could include their own theology but all talks had to be approved by World Wide Marriage Encounter. In the late 1970s Family Life Commission of Lancaster Conference in Pennsylvania, led by Henry and Marian Leaman, had the vision to pursue this and in 1980 Mennonite and Brethren Marriage Encounter was established. The theme is "to make a good marriage into a great marriage". Engaged Encounter is also part of Marriage Encounter and is very popular. Both Marriage Encounter and Engaged Encounter Weekends are still being given at Kenbrook Bible Camp, Lebanon, Pa. For information contact Marriage and Engaged Encounters, 134 E Mohler Church Rd., Ephrata, Pa 17522. Phone 717 569 5676.

CHAPTER 12

Silent Retreats and Spirituality

W hen I first received assurance of salvation just after my teen years I thought most of the people in the world were on their way to hell. It really bothered me but I did not know what to do about it. By reading selective tracts and Moody Colportage books it was rather clear most people were on the wrong way. I had peace with God and earnestly sought to do God's will. I slowly changed but I continued to desire to know and do God's will. I remember a time in Pax Germany that I realized I am friends with people who do not have quite the same religious beliefs I do. And before I left Pax Greece for home I had several very meaningful worship experiences in the Greek Orthodox Church. When I came home from three years of Pax in Europe I knew I was a different person but I wasn't sure if it was all for the good. I was more open and accepting of everybody without a theology to explain it. This continued in college as I did not take theology courses. I was briefly introduced to dispensational theology made popular by Scofield as well as Covenant theology but I didn't adhere to either. I think it was only after working at Provident Bookstore with access to many books and guidance from Lester Weber, my supervisor, that I began forming my own theology in earnest.

Spiritually my mentors have mostly been authors. During college several authors and their books that especially impacted me were Thomas Merton with No Man Is and Island, J. B. Philips with Your God Is Too Small, and Clarence Jordan with The Sermon on the Mount. But in forming my own theology I think I started with Anabaptism. I read HS Bender, The Anabaptist Vision; C.J. Dyck, Introduction to Mennonite History; John Miller, The Christian Way; John Howard Yoder, What Would You Do?; Walter Klaassen, Anabaptism, Neither Catholic nor Protestant and others. Anabaptism was somewhat basic for me.

My next period of growth or renewal came through what was known as the Charismatic Renewal Movement. My book mentors included Keith Miller, author of The Taste of New Wine, Bruce Larson, Larry Richards and John Wimber. Sara and I had friends involved in the movement and we attended seminars and charismatic worship services. Our spiritual life was touched and enhanced but we did not speak or pray in tongues.

After some years of the "taste of new wine" I read Celebration of Discipline by Richard Foster and realized the contemplative part of my spiritual life was never really developed! I was inspired by reading Celebration of Discipline but came to the conclusion that I don't really know what Foster is talking about and I wanted to know. So I decided to re-read the book slowly staying with a chapter until I at least partially understood and experienced the message of the chapter. It took me six or seven months to re-read the book and it probably effected me more than any other book I ever read. A few of the authors that were my mentors during this time were Henri Nouwen, Morton Kelsey, Elizabeth O'Conner and Eugene Peterson.

Some time later my friend and co-worker at Provident Bookstore, Nevin Horst, kept telling me about silent weekend retreats he was experiencing including a week of mostly silence. And Richard Foster referred to this as a spiritual discipline as did Marlene Kropf in her Gospel Herald articles. Finally in March of 1986 Sara and I went to Pendle Hill, a Quaker Retreat Center near Philadelphia for a three day weekend with the theme "Come to the Table, a Journal

Retreat in Silence". Our leader had some verbal input of course
with instructions, journal assignments, etc. and we had several al-
lotted times of sharing. We always ate together in silence which
was a unique and wonderful experience for me. The weekend was
so meaningful to us that for the next five or six years Sara and I attended at least one, usually two silent weekend retreats each year.
We had several very meaningful weekends at Dayspring Retreat
Center in Maryland, an outreach of the Church of the Savior in
D.C.

   During this time Lester Graybill, pastor of Forest Hills Mennonite Church, was a spiritual mentor for me for a year. And he
was enrolled at Shalem Institute for Spiritual Formation in Washington D.C. I was impressed with Lester's spirituality and decided
to enroll at Shalem also. I took a two year course mostly by correspondence and reading many books. This was before computers.
But there was also one week of residency at D.C. for each year.
These were somewhat out of my comfort zone but challenging
and meaningful. I experienced worship through chanting as well
as in silence. We worshiped by dancing which was enjoyable. And
I made friends. A friendship that continued for some years was
with Ken Nelson to whom I'll refer to in a bit. The two years required extensive reading some of which was beyond my grasp and
comprehension. Among the books that nurtured me were Open
Mind, Open Heart by Thomas Keating and The Art of Christian
Listening by Thomas Hart. In residency I had some unique prayer
times with Scripture in small groups and we had extended periods
of silence, like 24 hours. I think it was there that I was introduced
to a prayer by an ancient monk:

                Day by day dear Lord I pray
                Help me to
                see you more clearly

follow you more nearly
love you more dearly
Amen

This has been a meaningful prayer for me over the years.

I graduated in 1992 with a Certificate of Completion from Shalem Group Leaders Program for "leaders of Spiritual Formation groups". I did lead half a dozen or so spiritual formation prayer groups and was a mentor for a few people but it did not develop into a vocation for retirement as I thought it might.

Sara and I kept in touch with Ken Nelson and his wife Judy from Little Rock, Arkansas and later from Sedona, Arizona. We visited them at both places. When they visited us in November 1992 we discovered something very interesting. Judy as a little Lutheran girl in Minnesota and I as a little Amish boy in Pennsylvania prayed the same German prayer on our knees by our bedside every evening before retiring:

Müde bin Ich, gehe zu ruh
Schliese meine müde Augen zu
Ich bin noch schwach, Ich bin noch klein
Du grosser Gott wollst bei mir sein
Amen
(For English Translation see chapter one, page 3)

Many other people and events contributed to my spirituality along the way. I will mention two, Lester Weber and Harold Newell. Lester was my supervisor the first year I was at Provident Bookstore and then a book salesman who met me two or three times a year for many years and at book conventions. Harold Newell was also a book salesman whom I met in similar ways. Harold was Episcopalian and Lester was Mennonite. We almost always discussed theology and what it means to be a follower of Jesus whenever we met. When I retired from Provident in 1995 we realized we would not see each other any more. We decided to meet together at Yoders in New Holland for breakfast once a month and be "spiritual friends" for each other. And we decided to use the same daily devotional guide, Forward Day by Day an Episcopalian guide that Harold would provide. We began meeting sometime in 1996 and with very few exceptions met monthly for the next 18 years. Then for health reasons we didn't always meet and in April of 2015 Lester left this life and went on to the next. Harold and I still meet together for breakfast every two months. Meeting monthly with Lester and Harold had a profound effect on my spirituality.

I now see people as my fellow travelers from the cradle to the grave and I do not judge them. God is the judge and God is merciful and cares for them.

CHAPTER 13

Annual Peace Pilgrimage, Nazareth to Bethlehem

The Annual Peace Pilgrimage from Nazareth to Bethlehem in
Pennsylvania began in 1960 and has taken place every year
since that. It is a 10 mile walk on the second Saturday of December, a peace pilgrimage in honor of the journey of Mary and Joseph. Anywhere from 45-200 pilgrims usually participate largely
depending on the weather. It was started by the Quakers but now
supported by many peace organizations including Mennonite Central Committee. It is for people who feel strongly that war and
violence is never the best answer to conflict and differences. It is
not political.

I'm not sure when I first became aware of the Peace Pilgrimage. My first pilgrimage was probably in 1974 or 1975. I went
on an MCC sponsored bus from Lancaster and sat beside Floyd
Bartel, pastor of Bethel Mennonite Church in Lancaster. We were
the same age. According to Floyd's recent obituary he left for Kansas in 1976. At Bethlehem a bus takes everyone to the Moravian
Church in Nazareth. The pilgrimage begins from the church at
noon. There are three rest stops on the way. At Central Moravian
Church in downtown Bethlehem a few Christmas carols are sung.
From there everyone walks several blocks to Christ United Church
of Christ for hot soup and sandwiches, coffee and cookies. I always
really look forward to this. An appointed speaker then has a brief
talk on peace.

Since my first pilgrimage in 1974 or 1975 I have not missed more than four or five times so I have made the pilgrimage at least 35 times. I go for inspiration and because I want to be counted with those who feel strongly that war is not the best way to solve differences. As a follower of Jesus I personally feel I cannot participate in war because of the life example and teaching of Jesus. On this pilgrimage I always get inspiration from the people I meet and the speaker following the soup and sandwiches. For many years I'd look forward to meeting friends I hadn't seen for a year as Luke Martin who helped plan the event, John Stoner who came up with the phrase, "Let Christians agree not to kill other Christians" or something with that meaning. Also Becky Felton who would have a Provident Bookstore display and Howard McFarland whom Sara and I worked with sponsoring international students over Thanksgiving for many years. And I would usually meet some Franconia Mennonites that I knew. Except for Luke Martin none of these come anymore and I miss them. I hope to continue the pilgrimage at least three more times till I'm 90, Lord willing.

Following are some of the well known speakers over the years:

1978- Phillip Berrigan
1980- Robert Raines
1981- Richard McSorley, S.J.
1982- Ronald Sider
1989- John K. Stoner
1990- Myron Augsburger
1991- Marian Claassen Frantz
1992- C. Douglas Hostetter
1994- Jim Wallis
1999- John Dear, S.J.
2000- Gene Stoltzfus

2002- Susan Crane
2003- John Stoner
2004- Bob Edgar
2009- Dr. Rev. James Forbes
2015 Shane Clairborne
2016- Maryann Cusimano Love

If you live within several hours driving distance of Bethlehem, Pa. I invite you to join the Christmas Peace Pilgrimage the second Saturday in December. You need not pre-register although it is suggested you do. Information is available online for the time and place to meet in Bethlehem for Nazareth. Or you can call either 610-865-5204 or 610-433-6421. Should you happen to sprain an ankle or get overly tired during the walk a ride is available at all times. Come and we'll walk together for peace especially remembering Joseph and Mary and their pilgrimage to Bethlehem.

CHAPTER 14

Appalachian Trail

HARPER'S FERRY, WV, TO MAINE

The Appalachian Trail or AT is the l-o-o-o-o-n-g-e-s-t hiking only footpath in the world. It is two thousand one hundred ninety miles, 2,190, over mountains, rocks, roots, streams, rivers, ledges, hills, gullies and plateaus from Maine to Georgia mostly away from civilization. I walked this footpath.

100 years ago there was no such footpath or trail. Benton McKay, a dreamer, imagined the possibility, put his vision into writing and in 1921 had it published in a professional journey. In 1925 the Appalachian Trail Conference was formed and in the following decade the trail was designed and constructed mostly by volunteers. It officially opened in August of 1937. It was not well kept and was closed all of WWII. In 1948 Earl Shaffer, a war veteran, was the first person to hike the full distance but it wasn't until 1951 that it was really opened for its total 2,000 plus miles. In 1968 it became a National Park through 14 states.

I don't remember when I first heard of the AT. I do remember that as an adult I could not imagine anyone walking that distance. In July of 1988 I attended a spiritual retreat along with a friend Ken Mast at Kirkridge Retreat Center near Bangor, Pa. and the AT is nearby. I took a few steps on the trail in awe realizing its length when sure enough a thru hiker from Georgia came by and I talked with him. It was almost unbelievable for me that anyone would do that but there he was. It certainly wasn't anything I would ever do. I did enjoy hiking however and in 1993 my younger brother John invited me to Colorado and hike Pikes Peak with him. John's daughter Joy lived in Colorado at that time. I accepted the invitation so in the summer of 1993 Sara and I and our two youngest children, Irene and Herman drove to Rocky Mountain Mennonite Camp. The two girls Irene and Joy hiked to the Peak from the camp. John, Herman and I went to Manitou Springs where the cog rail begins and walked up a trail from there. When we arrived at over 13,000 feet elevation it was a rather steep ascent, some snow and the air was thin. John and I had to walk very, very, very slowly and rest every five minutes. But we made it. The next day while reflecting on the hike Herman commented that he would like to do the AT sometime. Then looking at me he said, "And I would like to do it with you, Dad." I had never envisioned of doing it, but a seed was planted. I got to thinking that the year Herman graduates, 1995, I would be 65 and could retire. So on Monday, May 8, 1995 Herman, Irene and I are at Harper's Ferry, West Virginia ready to walk to Maine.

That is Irene and I hoped to walk to Maine, ready or not. Herman had made a slight change in his major at college and had to take summer school in order to graduate. So the AT would not happen. However Irene, who was working at Mennonite Publishing House in Scottdale, PA, decided to resign, quit her job and walk with me. Herman would walk with us the first two weeks then come to Maine and finish with us. So on Monday morning Sara brought the three of us with our backpacks to Harper's Ferry, WV, said good-bye and left for home. I had a few tears when we said good-bye. I had never back-packed so basically everything I had was new: a new back-pack, sleeping bag, stove, tent, water bottles, water filter, shoes and socks. The back pack with contents weighed 50 lbs. I was not at all sure my decision to walk the AT was a good decision but there was no turning back. Sara was gone. Now I would take my first step of a thousand miles on this footpath to Maine carrying a 50 lb backpack.

Harper's Ferry is a beautiful town. We began our hike by crossing the Potomac River on a foot bridge then onto a towpath along the C&O Canal several miles then up South Mountain. We had a great overlook at the Potomac Weverton Rocks. I had somewhat tentatively planned the hike to Bennington, Vermont. Planned for the first day was a 10.4 mile hike to a side trail of .3 mile to Compton Gap Shelter. On the AT we passed a phone late afternoon in a park and I called home but Sara wasn't home. The 10 miles seemed long and we got very tired. We finally arrived at the side trail of .3 mile leading to a shelter. We assumed we missed the shelter because we thought we walked at least a half mile but then we arrived. Two men were already at the shelter. We were tired and hungry and had rice and hot chocolate for supper. I had wondered what it would be like to spend our first night in a shelter. Now this was it.

Our goal was to meet Sara at Caledonia State Park on Saturday about 60 miles from Harper's Ferry which we did. But I had a low point before we got there. We had access to a phone both Tuesday and Wednesday and I called home but Sara did not answer. Thursday I had no access to a phone and we slept at Penn Mar Campground. I did not know if Sara ever got home from Harper's Ferry. I experienced some homesickness, somewhat worried about Sara and thinking I was probably foolish leaving her alone while I did my thing of hiking. I did not sleep well. By staying at Penn Mar till after 9:00 on Friday morning we had access to a phone. I called home and Sara was not home. I called Mikes, our son and they weren't home either. So I called Nathans, our oldest son. They were home and all was well.

Sara met us at Caledonia State Park along Route 30 with clean clothes, a picnic lunch and week's supply of food for the three of us then again at Camp Hebron and along R309 near Allentown. At Camp Hebron Nathan and Sherilyn and their four children, Jeremiah, Janae, Jonathan, and Joshua also met us as well as Be'l King and Deb Leisey. At Rt 309 Be'l King was along again and Freda Miller. Herman had sent his shoes home with Sara at Camp Hebron and walked in his sneakers. He had serious blisters on both feet and decided to go home with them. Now it was just Irene and me. We missed Herman as he had somewhat kept us entertained and inspired. After Allentown Sara came three more times with clean clothes and food, Delaware Water Gap, R 17A by Bellvale NY and Kent, CT. Our six year old grandson Jeremiah was along at R 17A. At Kent Lawrence and Shirley King brought her. At Back-country Outfitters in Kent Irene and I exchanged our Whisper Lite stove that wasn't working for a new one, no charge, and I got a new back pack, no charge, because mine was coming apart at the seams. And Sara brought a new pair of hiking boots along for Irene. The next we would see Sara she would pick us up at North Adams, MA near the Vermont state line and take us to Jake and Lorraine Esh's home in Bennington, VT.

Plans were for Sara to meet us at the Catholic church along R 2 in North Adams around 2:00 pm. Irene and I arrived in North Adams around 11:00 so we had time for coffee, lunch, dry clothes, observe a wedding, etc. About 1:00 we sat along R 2 and waited. At 2:00 Sara, Be'l King and Marlene Hess came by and saw us. Irene and I with our back packs joined them and we drove the 20 miles or so to Jake and Lorraine Esh's home in Bennington. Jake was an old time Amish buddy of mine in Pennsylvania. We had an enjoyable time together. Jake and Sara gave me a haircut and I had a bath in a bath tub. Irene and Be'l played instruments and we sang together. On Sunday we went with Jake and Lorraine to the Alliance Church. Later Sara and I planned the rest of Irene and my hike, where Sara would send food and when to meet us at Baxter State

Park in Maine, the end of the AT. We also made arrangements with Jake and Lorraine that on Saturday, July 22 they would meet Irene and me on the trail near Bethel, ME and spend the weekend with us, which they did. Lorraine was from Maine. On Monday noon Sara, Be'l and Marlene had lunch with Irene and me at Friendly's in North Adams. They then left for Lancaster County and Irene and I headed north on the AT. The next time Sara would see us would be at Baxter State Park.

Now a bit about our walking. The trail was more difficult than I had anticipated. And I was not in shape. I weighed about 170 lbs. In the beginning I huffed and puffed going up steep inclines carrying my 45-50 lb back pack. But I lost weight rather rapidly and in about three weeks my body adjusted to the back pack just as it does when we gain weight. Both Irene and I got blisters on our feet that we had to contend with but usually we could still enjoy walking, at least I could. Irene couldn't always. And we encountered millions of mosquitoes; well we didn't count them but there were very many. I did some reflection of why God created mosquitoes without resolving it.

Irene and I had two goals everyday, to reach our destination and to enjoy the journey. In spite of the above paragraph we met both goals almost everyday. Irene contributed a lot to enjoying the journey while I emphasized more on reaching our destination but I truly did enjoy the journey also. I made a conscious effort to walk reverently, carefully, joyfully and gratefully every day and I pretty well succeeded.

After several weeks on the trail we discovered there was a trail culture and we were becoming part of the culture. Everyone has a trail name usually different from their real name. I was Pilgrim. When introductions were made we almost always used only our trail name. And of course we all were experiencing a very different lifestyle. We slept at a different place every night in a tent or a lean to shelter, never in a bed. We lacked most of the basic things we had at home, we had no readily available water for drinking or cooking or bathing or brushing teeth, no chairs to sit on, table to write on or eat off of, no refrigerator, phone, lights, no newspaper, radio or TV, no family or church, not just for a day but for weeks and months. Our usual responsibilities and possessions have all been left in the care of others. Except for surviving on the trail we are care-free, no other responsibilities.

Going north Irene and I made friends with others who were doing just what we were doing, walking the AT. And we felt surprisingly responsible for each other. We would share our joys and our pains and our goals. Every shelter had a journal where almost every hiker made an entry. This helped us keep contact with one another. Going north we became friends with Rainbow Rocker, Big Al, Gator, White Root, Lone Scout, Clog, Pathfinder, Packman, Moses, Jesus, Day Dreamer, Jingo, Duke and Dutchess, Peasly, Hammer and others.

I'll now share a few highlights or memorable experiences. The first one I'll share is when Irene and I stayed at Fahnestock State Park near Canopus Lake in New York. We spent Sunday morning their with our usual Sunday forenoon meditation and relaxing. However Irene went to a phone, called home and was informed Emily Joy Lapp, Mike and Karen's first child, our fifth grandchild, was born yesterday, June 10,1995 to very happy parents. We celebrated by each eating a hamburger.

A very memorable time going north was arriving and hiking above tree line in the White Mountains in New Hampshire, especially the first thirty minutes. It was almost a divine experience seemingly being on top of the world with 360 degree visibility looking around in every direction and seeing the mountains, hills, trees and valleys below. Hiking over the White Mountains for over a week was a wonderful experience. Something different and unique for the AT in the White Mountains are the eight stone huts built in the 1890s for hikers mostly above tree line and no roads nearby or leading to them. Local hikers make reservations for one or two nights and have everything taken care of. As the AT was being planned the trail by these huts now also became part of the AT. Arrangements were made that AT thru-hikers could stay in a hut for one night if room was available and work for their board and lodging by sweeping, making beds, cleaning, etc. Irene and I stayed in four of these huts. I'll share our experience at one, Lakes of the Clouds Hut near Mt. Washington. We arrived Sunday afternoon and were informed a storm was forecast for Sunday night and Monday. We decided to walk the 1 ½ hours to the peak and enjoy Mt. Washington in nice weather, which we did and walked back to our hut. A storm did come and it was very cold. We could only stay at Lakes of the Clouds Hut one night so we hiked to the top of Mt. Washington in the storm. It was one of the few times on the AT that I sensed was life threatening. We crawled on our hands and knees in an 80 mph wind with our back packs so we wouldn't be blown away. And it was sleeting and raining. We did of course reach the top where many visitors come, weather permitting. When we arrived only the proprietor was there. We could not stay overnight and were informed no one was permitted to be on the trails. So we checked our handbook and called a hostel in Gorham, Hikers Heaven, and made arrangements that Bruno the owner would come and get us for $45.00. Irene and I stayed at Hikers Heaven Monday night and all day Tuesday. White Root a thru-hiker was also there. On Wednesday forenoon Irene and I hitchhiked back to where the AT crosses R16 at Pinkham Notch and headed north toward Maine. We missed the section of the AT from Mt. Washington to Pinkham Notch and planned to do it on our way home from Maine which we did.

Crossing state lines was always exciting. But the day we crossed from New Hampshire to Maine was extra special. It was our ninth and last state line to cross. We saw our first bear and our first moose that day and we had only approximately 285 more miles to go. We were headed for Full Goose shelter about 5 miles into Maine for the night. Irene happened to be wearing her Ingram T-shirt she had gotten at Provident Bookstore. Ingram was a major book distributor. When we arrived at the shelter several men were already there. One of the men almost at once noticed Irene's T-shirt and threatened to burn it. We learned he was a former president of Baker & Taylor, another book distributor and a competitor or rival of Ingram. Two of the other people were father and son, Fred and Freddie, whom we had met on the trail previously several times. Fred was an author and politician from Toronto and a good friend of Newt Gingrich. Another man was "Gator", a 72 year old retiree, a former treasurer of "Arizona Highways" now living in Florida. We had met him various times. He had bought a quilt for his wife from Amanda Smucker in Lancaster County, Auntie Anne's mother. Here we were together in an open shelter in the Maine woods, far from any road or resident or phone in our sleeping bags- a former Baker and Taylor president, a former treasurer of the magazine "Arizona Highways", an author and politician and son from Toronto and Irene and I.

At home I had heard about Kennebec potatoes. Now in Maine we were approaching the Kennebec River and were at Pierce Pond, a beautiful lake. Our shelter was right by the lake or pond as such bodies of water were referred to in Maine. Irene and I both went swimming. Gator and Fred and Freddie were also there. Tomorrow we would cross the Kennebec River. There was a note by our shelter informing us that ahead a half mile off the trail at Harrison Cabin we can order a good breakfast so we did. It was a beautiful moonlight and we heard loons all night and some coyotes at our shelter. We heard them all night because a portion of the millions of mosquitoes we met on the AT kept us from sleeping much. However morning came and Irene and I went to breakfast. Gator from Florida and Fred and Freddie were also there. We had 12 pancakes each, two eggs, coffee and juice. I wrote in my journal they were the best pancakes I remember ever eating. And a wonderful setting. After breakfast we had an hours hike to the Kennebec River which we crossed in a canoe. Gator was with us. From the Kennebec we hiked to Caratunk where Sara had sent a package for us. We were approaching Monson and the 100 miles wilderness where we would meet Herman.

Irene and I were excited to walk in to Monson, Maine, as I had heard of it many times. Pearl Lapp's nephew, Daryl Witmer and his family live here. Daryl is in a wheel chair and Mel and Pearl often talked about him. I visited with him about a half hour. Irene and I stayed at Shaws with many other AT hikers. We each enjoyed a shower and a bath, a full evening dinner and morning breakfast along with sleeping in a bed. Friday forenoon Irene and I began our 100 mile "wilderness journey". It is called the "wilderness journey" because for 115 miles there are no public roads or access to supplies or telephone. There are many streams to cross, some mountains and two rivers. There are some logging roads in the wilderness however. And about thirty miles in the wilderness the AT crosses a logging road where Herman met us at 8:00 on Monday morning, parked his car and walked with us. It was great to have him with us again. Our hike through the wilderness was rather uneventful. We hiked about 20 miles each day and I could now walk up and down mountains without huffing and puffing. Somewhere on the trail I lost 30 pounds of body weight and no one ever reported of finding them. We were hoping Sara would be at Baxter State Park when we arrive but we had no communication with her since Monson just before entering the "wilderness".

On Friday morning we left the "wilderness" and were about a mile from Baxter State Park when a south bound hiker informed us there was someone along the trail in the Park waiting for us. We made that mile in record time and there was Sara waiting for us. Wow! She had driven 750 miles by herself to Millinocket where she spent the night on her cot by a lake and was at the trail on Friday afternoon when we arrived. After hugging each other, we shared our stories while enjoying the food Sara brought along. Sara then left for Millinocket again as she could not stay in the Park overnight but AT hikers could. A while after she left her brother David and his wife Fannie drove up to our lean-to shelter and surprised us. They had driven from Holmes County, Ohio so David could finish the hike with us on Saturday. This was a gesture I greatly appreciated. After visiting a while with David and Fannie they drove back to Millinocket also for the night.

At six o'clock on Saturday morning, Herman, Irene and I left our lean-to shelter and walked two miles up the trail where we had arranged to meet David and there he was waiting for us. We left the campground where David was at 7:15. Rain was forecast but we walked several hours in nice weather and it was very warm. David cut off his long pant legs. We had some great vistas as we were reaching the tree line and could see out over the scrubs. Soon after reaching tree line we walked into a thick cloud or fog and could not see anything. It was very rocky and we had to climb up over the rocks and small cliffs without being able to see around us. As we reached a plateau before the final peak it began to drizzle with almost a freezing rain. Herman and I reached the summit before Irene and David and cuddled under a big rock and ate our sandwiches till they arrived. We took several pictures at the Katadhin AT sign at the summit. It was an indescribable feeling of having reached our goal and having back packed over a thousand miles on a footpath over many mountains and streams to get here. On the return down the rain stopped for a while and we could see all around us. It was a great scene. And we discovered that we came up a narrow ridge or ledge without knowing it. It was more scary going down when we could see than it was climbing up while in a cloud. However, it again clouded up and rained for an hour or so. But it quit raining before we reached Katadhin Campground around 3:00. Sara and Fannie were there with lots of food spread out on a table under a roof. We had a great time eating and sharing food with other hikers. I had taken a shower and put on clean dry clothes Sara had brought along. It's impossible to describe how good that felt knowing I would not have to put on wet hiking clothes again in the morning. Other than the Mahoosuc Notch, a mile long gully or canyon full of fallen boulders, Mt. Katadhin is probably the most difficult hike of the 2,000 mile trail.

We said good bye to some of our hiker buddies then Sara took us and our backpacks to the "wilderness" where Herman had his car. We saw a moose just before arriving at his car. Herman and Irene drove to Gorham NH yet for the night. Sara and I got a motel at Bangor, attended a very meaningful service at a nearby Episcopal Church on Sunday morning then drove to Gorham also. Be'l King and Deb Leisey were with Irene at the Colonial Comfort Inn to welcome us. Herman had left for home in the morning so he could work all week. On Monday morning Sara took Irene and me to Pinkham Notch and Irene and I got on the AT and hiked the 13 miles to Mt. Washington that we had missed on our hike north. We got to the summit soon after 4:00 and Sara and Be'l and Deb were there to meet us. Our hike was completed! Irene left with Be'l and Deb. I went with Sara. The five of us slept with a hiker friend in Hanover. On Tuesday Sara and I stopped in to see Jake and Lorraine Esh again in Bennington, Vermont, to report on our hike and thank them again for how they helped us. We arrived home in Buena Vista soon after 9:00 pm. A wonderful three months for me. I wrote the following paragraph in my journal:

"A trip of a thousand miles begins with the first step." Herman, Irene and I are in Harper's Ferry, W.V., about to take our first step on the Appalachian Trail (AT) and walk 1,000 miles to Maine.

The sign at Pen-Mar reminds us we have many miles to go. Pen-Mar was a low point for me.

Everyday we had two goals, get to our destination and enjoy the journey. Here Irene and I are enjoying the journey.

Laurence and Shirley King brought Sara to Kent, Connecticut with food and clean clothes for Irene and me. We enjoyed eating pizza.

Hiking above tree line in the White Mountains of New Hampshire was a great, worshipful experience for me.

The Mahoosuc Notch in Maine is the most difficult one mile of the AT.

Because of no roads in the 100 mile wilderness section of the AT in Maine there are no bridges. You walk through the rivers.

Sara's brother David on the AT walking to Mt. Katahdin.

We did it! A very emotional moment! Omar, Irene, Herman.

Heading south to Georgia on the AT. Ruby Miller and Irene walked with me the first week. Herman joined me on the third week and walked most of the rest of the AT south with me.

Top: *Five of the grandchildren, Jonathan, Janae, Jessica, Jeremiah, and Joshua with their parents Sherilyn and Nathan were at Harper's Ferry to say goodbye to Grandpa on May 8, 2000. In 2016 Joshua hiked the complete AT.*

Right: *Shenandoah National Park has some extra accommodations as well built shelters and bear poles. I am in the process of hanging my food on a bear pole.*

Mel and Pearl Lapp brought Sara to meet Herman and me on the AT south of Roanoke, VA. They brought a week's supply of food, clean clothes and treated us to a wonderful meal at a restaurant.

Damascus, Va. is an AT friendly town and The Place is a popular place for hikers to stay. From here Herman went home with Sara and Irene, flew to Arizona and drove his pick up back to the AT. I walked by myself for eight days.

Jessie, Jason and Sharon Troyer from Crossville, Tennessee brought a meal plus a week's supply of food to Newfound Gap near Gatlinburg, Va. for Herman and me.

This is Springer Mountain, Georgia where I completed my 2,000 mile hike of the AT at age 70. Herman did the southern part with me.

"I've probably never experienced as many mosquito bites or perspired as much in three months as I did doing the AT. And I've never worked harder or lacked as many conveniences. But I've done very little in life that I've enjoyed as much."

HARPER'S FERRY, WV, TO GEORGIA

After hiking from Harper's Ferry, WV to Maine I often tell people I rested five years and when I was 70 decided to hike the southern half of the trail from Harper's Ferry to Georgia. And I did it.

On May 8, 2000 Sara brought Irene, our daughter, Ruby Miller, Sara's niece from Ohio and me to Harper's Ferry where I would begin walking the 1,000 miles to Georgia on a footpath. Irene and Ruby would accompany me for about a week and Herman would join me in a little over two weeks. Nathan, our oldest son and his wife Sherilyn and five children, Jeremiah, Janae, Jonathan, Joshua, and Jessica followed us to Harper's Ferry to see us take our first steps. I had the same walking stick I used to walk to Maine. At the AT Headquarters and store walking sticks were available for $1.00 each and Nathan bought one for each of the children. Sometime before noon Irene, Ruby and I began walking south on the AT. Nathans and Sara headed for home.

The first night we three hikers slept in a lean-to shelter having seen a big black snake and a turtle on the trail. The second night I had made arrangements to meet Freda Miller, Sara's niece living in Catlett, Virginia, at Bear's Den Hostel, a beautiful hostel close to the trail. We hikers were very tired. Freda and several of her friends spent the night at the hostel and we had a very nice evening together. Be'l King and Deb Lisey picked up Irene on Friday forenoon as Irene had commitments for Friday eve. Ruby and I walked another day and Sara came with food and clean clothes for me. Ruby went home with her. My first night alone a bear walked close by as I was eating my supper outside the shelter.

I got to walk the AT through the Shenandoah National Park approximately 100 miles by myself. I of course met many other people. The shelters in the Shenandoah are mostly made of stone and have a bear pole to hang up your food so bears cannot get it. The AT crosses the Skyline Drive many times. Some of the interesting people I met in the Park were the Pennsylvania Dutchmen, four Mennonite boys from Bernville, north of Reading, PA. I visited with them about an hour. They walked here from Georgia and are headed for Maine. Sara and I got to visit them in their home community in 2001. Soon after entering the Park I met Just Jim, an elderly man from Norfolk, VA walking to Waynesboro. He gets his milk at Yoder's Dairy and knows the Mennonites there. We became friends and often walked together. And I met a group of seven women several times and chatted with them. They are professional women who have been doing a week on the AT together for several years. And Sara and Irene came to see me and brought clean clothes and a week's supply of food. I also got two adjustable walking sticks from Irene and sent my one walking stick home with her. Almost all long distant hikers now have two adjustable poles or sticks. The Pennsylvania Dutchmen had me try theirs and said how helpful they are. So I had Irene bring me some. I enjoyed my walk through the Shenandoah very much. But I looked forward to meeting Herman and walking with him.

This school year Herman was teaching in a Jr High Native American school near Ganado, Arizona. He figured if he leaves right after school he could meet me on the trail by May 24. I had made a potential schedule all the way to Springer Mountain, Georgia before leaving home and on May 24 I would be at Priest Shelter just south of R56 in Virginia. I had not heard from Herman since I was on the trail but Sara informed me earlier in the week Herman was hoping to get to the trail on Wednesday afternoon or evening. I arrived where the trail crosses R 56 at 11:45, waited till 1:00 and

decided to walk the five miles to Priest Shelter, up a 3,000 feet ascent. I arrived at the shelter at 4:30. At 6:00 I decided to cook my
dinner. The shelter was getting full but I reserved a place for Herman. He arrived at 9:30 and I was very glad to see him. He told me
Mom, Sara, picked him up at the Baltimore airport on Tuesday. He
spent a night at home in Buena Vista then drove to Eastern Mennonite High School in Harrisonburg, VA and had his buddy Dave
Becker bring him to the trail.

After walking and talking with Herman on the trail several
days Sara and Irene met us at US 501 by the James River and we
got a motel in Buena Vista, VA. At the Grace Brethren Church on
Sunday Sara and I met an elderly lady who said she helped cook
for the Mennonite Disaster Service, MDS, men in 1969 after the
huge flood. I was with the group she cooked for. Paul Smucker,
John Smoker, Naaman Yoder and I from Sandy Hill Mennonite
Church were there a few days helping in August of 1969. Irene and
Sara went home by EMHS to get the pick-up Herman left there on
his way to the trail.

Before leaving home friends of Sara and mine, Bill and Judy
Houser and David and Martha Clymer informed us that their
friends Merv and Rachel Frey from Greencastle, PA were hiking
the trail from Georgia to Maine and we would meet them. We had
no contact with them and had never met them. For the past week
or so we thought we might meet them and hoped we could identify
them if we met. Several days south of Buena Vista, VA on a cold
rainy day Herman and I were eating lunch in a shelter with half a
dozen other hikers. We used only our trail names in brief introductions. Herman suspected the one couple was Merv and Rachel Frey
and sure enough it was. We had a very nice visit. Their trail names
were Pioneer and Rider.

Going north my body had more extra fat it could use as
needed than it did going south. One morning Herman and I de-

cided to get up early and hike several miles to a McDonalds near
the AT for breakfast. Before eating I went to a nearby truck stop
to a phone and called Sara. After talking a while I got light headed
and realized I needed to sit down. So I informed Sara and hung up.
I should have called her back but I didn't. I was not getting enough
calories which was the cause of getting light-headed. After a good
McDonald's breakfast I was okay.

Herman was dating a girl in Arizona and was keeping in
touch with her by occasional phone calls along the trail. After our
McDonald's breakfast he decided he would like to go five miles
beyond the shelter we planned to stay for the night and hike to
Catawba for an all you can eat meal and phone availability. So I
had a relaxing and very scenic walk alone. I went by McAfee Knob,
a well-known outlook featured on many calendars and postcards
but I had no one to take my picture on the high extended ledge. I
also had an interesting bear experience. The bushes beside the trail
were about three feet high and in front of me several hundred yards
a perhaps half-grown bear cub crossed the trail. I stopped assum-
ing the mother would follow. I waited five minutes or so and no
mother bear. I said a prayer and walked on. I felt very relieved when
I was well past. We saw many more bear going south than going
north. One day in the Smokies we saw six bear as we were walking.

Another bear story concerns Herman. There are very few
outhouses on the AT. You carry a small spade and the woods are
your outhouse. Herman was having his "outhouse" time under a
tree in the woods. He thought several times he heard a bear but
could not locate it. As we were leaving we looked back and there
was a bear in the tree under which he had been sitting.

Somewhere in southern Virginia I chatted a while with a
young man from Scotland on the trail. I mentioned that while I
enjoyed backpacking this was my last long distant hike. I said it
was not fair to my wife to have her alone for such long periods of

time. And because of her arthritic feet she cannot hike with me. He informed me of a one thousand year old trail in Spain on which he hiked several hundred miles. On that trail it would be possible for Sara my wife to have a rented car and frequently meet me. Before we parted he predicted I would hike that trail sometime.

It was Thursday morning June 1, when I ended my phone conversation with Sara by hanging up because I was light-headed. The following Saturday we had arranged that she and Mel and Pearl Lapp would meet Herman and me on the trail near New Castle, VA at 11:00 am. Herman and I had an eight mile hike to our planned meeting place and we arrived at 10:50. Just as we arrived, Mel, Pearl, and Sara pulled in and tooted their horn after a six hour drive from home. We were delighted to see each other. Mel and Pearl treated us to a great lunch at a restaurant in New Castle. After a nice visit Herman and I headed south on the trail with clean clothes and a weeks supply of food in our packs. Mel, Pearl and Sara headed north for their six hour drive home.

Two weeks after Mel and Pearl met us, Sara and Irene came to Damascus, VA. We all slept in "The Place", a hikers hostel on Friday night and in a motel in Abingdon on Saturday night. After hiking on the AT about a month with lots of time for reflecting and some phone calls, Herman decided to leave Arizona and live in Pennsylvania again for a while. So Sunday morning at Damascus about 10:00 Herman headed home with Sara and Irene. His plans were to fly to Arizona from Baltimore on Monday, say good-bye to his friends, bring Jake, his dog, and all his belongings with his pick-up back to the trail at Erwin, TN. So on Sunday afternoon I headed south alone on the trail for my weeks hike of just over 116 miles to Erwin, TN. The north bound thru-hikers were all further north by now so I didn't meet many hikers. I think two different days I saw no one.

Farther north we had met many hikers, mostly north bound thru-hikers but also section hikers and a few south bound thru-hikers. Often the shelters were full. We got to know several south bound section hikers fairly well. And we made some friends by just spending a long evening and a night together at a shelter. Sometimes their trail name revealed something about them. I'll mention some: Buckeye Bob, Stoneman, Mushroom, Special Agent, Green Jeans, Bugger, No Fuel, Midlife Crisis, Horsetrot, Colorado, Lone Star, Candyman, Leap Frog, Apple, Socrates, Opa, Amtrak, Soul Man, Firekeeper, Silver Bear and Dakota.

One special time for me while doing this southern part of the AT alone was Saturday night and Sunday forenoon at a shelter in the Cherokee National Forest. I was far away from any road or civilization. I had not heard from Sara or Herman since a week ago at Damascus. The forenoon alone with God in the forest was really special. On Sunday afternoon I walked through a very heavy downpour of rain for a half hour before reaching my Sunday night shelter.

On Monday morning I had only a little over four miles from where I slept to Nolichucky Hostel near Erwin where I hoped to meet Herman. I arrived at Nolichucky Hostel soon after 9:00 and reserved two beds for the night. I waited an hour till a phone was available and called Sara. She said Herman was planning to be at Troyers at Crossville for Sunday and drive to Erwin on Monday. He arrived around 6:00 and we went uptown and ate at Wendys. Tuesday morning we headed south on the AT hoping to reach Hot Springs about 70 miles south on Friday which we did. We had a wonderful day at Hot Springs Friday eve and Saturday. We got our week's food supply Sara sent us and got our permit to hike through the Smokies. We left late afternoon for our short three mile hike to our Saturday night shelter.

One of my few low points on the AT was Wednesday night before Hot Springs arriving at Little Laurel Shelter. We had walked through heavy rain which was not unusual but somehow the rain got into my backpack which was unusual and everything not in plastic bags was soaked including my sleeping bag. It was cold and I did not know what to do. I felt like crying. Herman came to my rescue. He gave me his cozy sleeping bag. I had a pair of dry trousers in a plastic bag in my backpack which he put on. He used our canvas tent as a cover and claims he slept fairly well.

It was exciting to reach the entrance to the Great Smoky Mountain National Park 780 miles from Harper's Ferry. The Smoky Mountains are considered a northern hemisphere rain forest. We did have rainy and foggy days but also very scenic and nice weather days. We had arrangements to meet the Troyers at R 441 east of Gatlinburg at New Found Gap in the Smokies. Herman and I noticed we were a bit ahead of schedule and also saw there was a five mile trail from the AT to Mt. Laconte before New Found Gap. Mt. Laconte was a familiar name to Sara's family. Sara's father and grandfather had hiked it and all of Sara's brothers and sisters. And sometime later Sara and I hiked it with considerable difficulty. So Herman and I took the opportunity to hike it again. We were hungry hoping we could buy something to eat at the top but only raisins and Hershey bars were available. We relaxed sitting on chairs at the Visitors Center and ate raisins and Hershey bars. The next day we met Jesse, Jason and Sharon Troyer, Herman's cousins. They had a wonderful picnic lunch for us and brought our weeks food supply that Sara had sent to them at Crossville. They hiked a portion of the trail with us before returning to Crossville.

The day after leaving Troyers we spent some time at Clingman's Dome, the highest point on the AT, 6,642 feet. On Monday we completed our hike through the Great Smokey Mountain National Park at Fontana Dam in Tennessee. This was the day we saw six bear. The Fontana Dam shelter where Herman and I stayed two nights is nicknamed "The Hilton" because of its size and accommodation. And here at the Hilton Jesse Troyer and Jonathan

Pinkham came to do the trail with us for four days. However due to a death in their church of an elderly man they left us after a two days hike at Nantahala Outdoor Center in Wesser, NC. We had an enjoyable time together at the Center and celebrated Jesse's 25th birthday there.

After Jesse and Jonathan left us Herman and I of course headed for Springer Mountain. The shelter we expected to stay on our third night in Georgia had tape all around it marked "No Entry" and signs saying there was dangerous bear activity. So we walked some miles further to a shelter that was a little over a mile off the AT. As we approached the shelter we noticed a bear on the trail close to the shelter eating something on the ground. We stood there just a bit and the bear looked up. He evidently did not like the way we looked and walked off. Upon investigating we discovered apparently a hiker had left some surplus food in the shelter for the next hikers. The bear had entered the shelter, torn off the attachment with the food and was just starting to eat it when we intruded. The bear was eating the first of three packs of something. I think it was oatmeal but I'm not sure anymore. Herman and I were very glad for the other two packs because we were basically out of food. The bear hung around the shelter all evening, sometimes appearing on one side then later on another side.

Sometime after we arrived, two other hikers came to the shelter, sisters, one living in Bethel, Alaska and one in Florida. The one from Alaska was very afraid of bear, being familiar mostly with grizzly bear. We of course made sure we had no food, toothpaste or anything that might attract a bear in the shelter. Like most shelters, this shelter was three-sided and had an open front. We hung our backpacks on tree branches as usual. Herman and I carried twigs and small branches and put them in front of our open shelter so supposedly if the bear decided to come during the night, we would hear him. Herman and I each had a club and slept somewhat in front on one side and the girls in back on the other side. We of course were going to protect them but we never heard or saw the bear.

Alive and well on Friday morning Herman and I said good bye to the two sisters, hiked our mile to the AT then hiked over three mountains to the Walasi-Yi Center at Neels Gap. The Center is a large stone building in a beautiful setting in the Chattahooche National Forest. The AT actually goes through an archway of the building. And its a great Outfitter and Gift Store with some groceries and snack food. Nice picnic tables are outside making it a real haven for hikers. It happened that a GPTV, Georgia Public Television, crew was doing some interviews and they interviewed me about the bear by the shelter. So I was on GPTV sometime. They later sent me a video which I still have.

But the great thing for Herman and me that happened here at the Walasi-Yi Center was that Irene met us there to walk the remainder of the AT with us. After Irene arrived we got a motel room at Blairsville and Saturday morning Irene parked her car near Neels Gap. We hiked up Blood Mountain from where we had a great view then had a relaxing Sunday afternoon hike. We had more mice than usual at our last shelter also a storm and a leak in the roof. But on Monday at 10:00 we arrived at the Terminus at Springer Mountain! It was hazy but we took several pictures and celebrated by eating our snacks. I had now walked all of the Appalachian Trail from Maine to Georgia!!

We still had 8.8 miles down the mountain to the Visitors Center by Amicalola Falls where we hoped faithful Sara would be waiting for us. And she was. Sara had been with relatives Paul and Miriam Zook and Robert, Rhoda and Clara Miller in Abbeyville SC over the weekend and now was here for us. It was wonderful. We hikers took hot showers, got into clean clothes and ate a picnic lunch Sara had brought along. Before leaving we drove to the top of

Amicalola Falls just to see them. We then drove to Neels Gap, got Irene's car and had a light supper at Millie's Restaurant. Herman and Irene headed for Erwin where Herman had his pick-up. Sara and I got a very nice motel room at Franklin NC where I trimmed my beard and shaved. When we arrived home on Tuesday eve July 25 we had a phone message informing us our ninth grandchild, Jerilyn Grace, was born this morning and everyone is well.

This ends my account of walking the longest hiking only footpath in the world. Did I learn anything? I think I did.

- I learned that my home church, my family, my home community and the world can get along without me. I need to remember this.
- I learned to respect my body and be thankful in a new way for a strong, healthy body
- I learned new ways of praying and worshiping
- I gained a new respect for my wife, her faithfulness and her abilities
- I learned again that joy and fulfillment in life are not dependent on an accumulation of things.

Walking the Appalachian Trail was truly an unforgettable event in my life.

CHAPTER 15

Mennonite World Conference

The first Mennonite World Conference, MWC, I attended was in Karlsruhe, Germany in August 1957. I was just completing my Pax term and I wrote about it in chapter 6, PAX, under, "Workcamp, Mennonite World Conference" and I won't add additional information. I just know I was delighted to have the privilege of being there. Harold Bender from Goshen, Indiana was president of MWC at Karlsruhe.

In August of 1962 I attended Mennonite World Conference in Kitchener, Ontario. I kept no diary or journal in 1962 so I write from memory. I was accompanied by Sara Ellen Miller to whom I was engaged to be married. Waldemar Eger from Germany whom I had met at Bienenberg Bible School in Switzerland and now a student at Eastern Mennonite College took us in his vehicle. We stopped to visit my brother John and his wife Floy and family on our way at Port Allegany in northern Pennsylvania. About the only thing I remember well from Conference is seeing and hearing Harold Bender give a passionate speech. He was passionate in desiring unity among Mennonites, especially between General Conference and Old Mennonites in the United States and Canada. And Harold was aware as we all were that he was dying of cancer. He died about six weeks later. Harold was president of MWC at Kitchener.

In July 1978 I with Sara and our four children attended MWC in Wichita, Kansas. As a family we had driven to Denver,

Colorado to attend the five day Christian Booksellers Convention there. On our way home from Denver to Wichita I remember two incidents quite well. The first was a flat tire. In order to get the jack and the spare tire many things needed to be taken out of the station wagon. I set my briefcase on the bank and somehow left it there. Among the contents were names and addresses of ex-Paxers and the names of all the villagers in Tsakones, Greece where I lived for two years.

The other incident was we followed a pick-up truck, with Alberta license plates, made into a camper with the title THE REMPLES above the door in back. This was of interest to us because we assumed they are Mennonites going to MWC. And I had a niece, Donna Lapp, married to Peter Remple living in Alberta. So when they stopped at a small restaurant we did also. And sure enough it was Peter Remple's twin brother Paul, married to Joanne Coffman Remple from Harrisonburg, Virginia. It was wonderful to meet them.

I don't remember much of Conference. I visited at length with some European Mennonites including Samuel Gerber from Switzerland and I think Willy Peterschmidt from France. I remember Samuel expressed his concern about a lack of reverence and all the noise and informality. Sara and I attended a Pax reunion there with a dozen or more ex-Paxers which was very meaningful. Two people shared the presidency at MWC in Wichita, Million Belete from Ethiopia and Charles Christiana from Indonesia.

In July of 1990 I attended MWC in Winnipeg, Manitoba. While I kept no diary or journal covering Kitchner and Wichita MWC, at Winnipeg, I did keep a journal. At customs in Winnipeg I checked "Business" as my purpose for coming and had difficulty getting through. I think Jack Scott from Mennonite Publishing House came to help me. I should have checked "Tourist" rather than "Business". At Conference I worked at the Provident Book-table every day which I enjoyed. According to my journal three couples from my home church, Sandy Hill Mennonite, were at Winnipeg MWC: Sam and Naomi Yoder, Lawrence and Shirley King, and Mel and Pearl Lapp. Other people I met were Werner and Grace Will, Miriam Krantz, Verna Miller and John Kanagy. Two workshops I was able to attend were led by Eleanor Kreider and Gene and Mary Herr. Ross Bender from Goshen, Indiana was president of MWC at Winnipeg.

On Tuesday July 7, 2009 Sara and I were at the Philadel-phia airport connecting with TourMagination people headed for MWC in Asuncion, Paraguay. Our friends Lester and Lydia We-ber were on the same tour. And it turned out our seat mate Eliza-beth Jacobs from Lancaster was also on the tour and we became good friends. We changed planes at Miami then Buenos Aires, Argentina and arrived at Asuncion around noon Thursday, July 9.

After spending the night in Excelsior Hotel our group had a three day trip to the Chaco by way of the 300 mile long Trans-Chaco Highway. Ever since my Pax days I was quite interested in both the Chaco and the Highway. Some of my Pax friends helped build the Trans-Chaco Highway from 1956-1961. Before that there was no road to the Chaco. And following World War II Peter and Elfrieda Dyck accompanied thousands of Russian Men-nonite refugees to Paraguay many of which settled in the Chaco. Reading Henry's Red Sea by Barbara Smucker and Up From the Rubble by Peter and Elfrieda Dyck intensified my interest about the Chaco. It was almost too good to be true that I was actually now driving on the Highway and visiting the Chaco. We visited two colonies, Menno and Fernheim. Having read Like a Mustard Seed, Mennonites in Paraguay by Edgar Stoesz and Paraguay, A Tour Guide With Special Emphasis on the Mennonites by Erwin

Boschman I had expected the Chaco to be even more advanced then it was. Filadelfia where our group stayed two nights had very few paved roads and the old part of the hotel where Sara and I stayed had no hot water. But there was no poverty and the average income of the people in the Chaco was much greater than the rest of Paraguay. At home during the 60's and 70's Sara and I sometimes hosted MCC Trainees and on August 13, 1970 we had hosted Elsie Penner from the Chaco. Upon inquiring I discovered Elsie was living in Filadelfia and might be at the large Mennonite Church some of us planned to attend. Sara and I really wanted to meet Elsie and prayed about it. The Mennonite Church building was large seating 500 people. When there was opportunity for introductions we discovered Elsie was right in back of us. We became friends again and Elsie and Sara sat with each other during many of the Conference sessions.

After the Chaco our tour group spent two days east of Asuncion. We drove to Brazil and toured the famous Iguazu Falls, visited the Leprosy Hospital Compound and stopped at the road that leads to a nearby Beachy Amish settlement with a Health Clinic. Sara's niece Ruby Miller worked there for many years. We talked with Naomi Eichorn who knew Ruby and lived at the place we stopped.

The next five days we enjoyed participating in the many conference activities. I was especially impressed how orderly and quickly over 5,000 people were fed. On Wednesday morning two boys, Lars Ackerson and Jon Spicher, shared about their six month bicycle trip to the Conference. They left Harrisonburg, Virginia on January 6, biked through Mexico, Central and South America to Paraguay. It was exciting to meet old friends from home and from far away. Among others we met Bill and Thea Klassen from Kansas, Arno Thimm from Germany now living in Holland, La-Mar and Kathryn Stauffer and Harold and Esther Kraybill from home. I enjoyed the well attended Pax Seminar. In the general sessions open for everyone, I knew only a few of the speakers, Nancy Heisey, Larry Miller and Elizabeth Soto. In the many workshops I took I knew quite a few of the leaders, Conrad Kanagy, Richard Showalter, Eleanor and Alan Kreider, Tom Finger and Loren Johns. The singing and music at the main sessions were wonderful and inspirational.

Very early Sunday morning a group of about 40 of us including Lester and Lydia Weber left for a five day tour of Peru. We spent a day at Lima then flew to Cusco. Bethany Geib, a coworker of mine at Provident Bookstore and a friend was now a school teacher and missionary in the outskirts of Cusco. Sara and I spent a night and a day with her which was informative and enjoyable. Our tour group all took the train to Machu Pichu, ancient ruins from the 15th century high in the Andes Mountain. Machu Pichu and the Iguazu Falls were two of the most impressive places we visited on our tour. But the purpose of the tour was MWC. We arrived home safely Friday July 24. Nancy Heisey from the US was president of MWC at Asuncion.

The last and 6th MWC I attended was July 2015 at Harrisburg, Pa, close to home. Sara and I commuted every day. Our pastor, Mick Sommers from Ridgeview Mennonite Church rented a 15 passenger van and provided our transportation. Sara's sister Irma and her husband John Miller from Ohio were at our home for the week and commuted with us. Sara and I now attend Ridgeview Mennonite Church since October 2014 after having been at Sandy Hill for almost 50 years. It was not an easy change but we felt it was right for us.

The singing and the worship at Assembly were exhilarating everyday. Meeting many new and old friends made it very worthwhile to be there. The large uniquely furnished prayer room was a great place for reflection, solitude and prayer. The Global Village was also a nice place to sit, relax, meet and talk with people. Sara spent a lot of her time there. We heard many inspiring messages by interesting and dedicated people of which I'll only mention two. Kevin Ressler was one of the Young Anabaptist speakers. I found him of particular interest because he was a local African American from Lancaster. Bruxy Cavey from Ontario spoke on the final night of the week. I found him interesting probably more for his humor and his dress but I felt he had an excellent message.

Because meeting friends was such an inspiration to me I'll mention a few. First of all it was a pleasure and a delight to see and say "hi" to two of our granddaughters at various times, Ellen and Kelly Lapp. They are the daughters of Michael and his wife, Karen. The granddaughters were enjoying MWC with their church friends. It was an inspiration to talk with and take a workshop with Chester Wenger 97 years old, a former missionary. Miriam Krantz showed me her picture album from Nepal where she has lived for over 50 years and expects to live there the rest of her life. I met Ruthild Foth from Germany who I think has been at 10 or more Mennonite World Conferences. I met Bethany Geib whom Sara and I had visited in Peru and Reta Halteman Finger whom I mentioned in chapter seven. And old friends I seldom see, Harvey Yoder, J Mark and Emma Frederick, Mike and Mattie Mast plus local friends. It was well worth taking off a week from my retirement job and pay what it cost to attend MWC for a week.

The next MWC will be in Indonesia in 2021. Nelson Kraybill from USA is now president of MWC. Danisa Ndlovu from Zimbabwe was president of MWC at Harrisburg.

The following may be of interest to you.

I attended the six bolded Conferences.

MENNONITE WORLD CONFERENCES

DATE	LOCATION	PRESIDENT
1. June 1925	Basel, Switzerland	Christian Neff, Germany
2. Aug/Sept 1930	Free City of Danzig	Christian Neff, Germany
3. June/July 1936	Amsterdam and Witmarsum Netherlands	Christian Neff, Germany
4. Aug 1948	Goshen, Ind. and Newton, Kan.	Peter Hiebert, US
5. Aug 1952	Basel and Zurich Switzerland	Harold Bender, US
6. Aug 1957	**Karlsruhe, Germany**	Harold Bender, US
7. Aug 1962	**Kitchner, Ont.**	Harold Bender, US
8. July 1967	Amsterdam, Netherlands	Erland Walter, US
9. July 1972	Curitiba, Brazil	Erland Walter, US
10. July 1978	**Wichita, Kansas**	Million Belete, Ethiopia Charles Christiana, Indonesia
11. July 1984	Strasbourg, France	Million Belete, Ethiopia Charles Christiana, Indonesia
12. July 1990	**Winnipeg, Manitoba**	Ross Bender, US
13. Jan 1997	Calcutta, India	Raul Garcia, Argentina
14. Aug 2003	Bulawayo, Zimbabwe	Mesach Krisetya, Indonesia
15. July 2009	**Ascuncion, Paraguay**	Nancy Heisey, US
16. July 2015	**Harrisburg, Pennsylvania**	Danisa Ndlovu

CHAPTER 16

Retirement

My retirement started March 31, 1995 after having worked at Provident Bookstore twenty-seven years. The first thing I did of course was walk the Appalachian Trail to Maine. After doing the AT I had three months of mail to go through and pursue potential job possibilities. I worked on putting together an AT photo album. After an interview with Clair Smoker at Good Foods I began working there two days a week on September 5, 1965. Good Foods is located in Honey Brook, Pa. and buys baking mixes, cooking oils, and liquid sweeteners as molasses and pancake syrup in very large quantities, repackages them and sells them wholesale to stores and bakeries. They mix a lot of Auntie Anne's pretzel dough. I spent considerable time working in the cooking oil room where Michael my son was supervisor. I was impressed at Michael's skill at doing his work well. I enjoyed my work at Good Foods but it was hard work at times with a need to work fast so as not to slow down production.

I had a friend from church, Jim Hertzler, who had a retirement job at NAPA and really liked it. I had applied for a job at NAPA at Gap upon my completion of the AT. When NAPA had a job opening the end of February I took it after six months at Good Foods. NAPA was a good retirement job for me and with various breaks I worked there a total of 12 years. NAPA, National Automotive Parts Association but better known as NAPA Auto Parts, was founded in 1925 and delivers automotive replacement parts, accessories and service items in the US, Canada and Mexico. Marvin and Sherry Stoltzfus owned and managed NAPA at Gap and Marvin was a great person under whom to work. We drivers each had a NAPA pick-up and made deliveries within a 15/20 mile radius of Gap which I really enjoyed. After a year or so Marvin built a new large NAPA store and warehouse and sold it to NAPA of York, PA under whom I then worked. Basically only retired people, usually men, work as delivery drivers because NAPA only pays minimum wage for this job. Drivers usually work because they enjoy it and can live on minimum wage.

In the summer of 1999 my friend Harold Newell informed me that his friend Joe had an office supply business, Johnstone Supply, near Exton, Pa and needed two part time drivers. Pay was much better than NAPA so I decided to take it. I enjoyed the work and got to know the country between Quakertown and West Chester that I was not familiar with. And drivers had work when not making deliveries which was better than just sitting and waiting for a delivery at NAPA. However, a big job Johnstone Supply bid on did not develop. After six months work was slow and I was told to see if I could get another job. I called NAPA and sure enough they were looking for a driver. So in January of 2000 I was back at NAPA again. I worked three days a week till May 1 then I quit so I could do the southern part of the Appalachian Trail. From May 8 to July 25 I was on the AT, most of the time with Herman.

The month of August after the AT I renovated the "halfway house" at home and put new drainage connections to the septic tank with help of course. The "halfway house" is what we call the entrance where one can then enter either the old original house built around 1895 or the part added in 1964. We put in new floor and ceiling. Merv Stoltzfus helped. Nathan did the drywall. And Reuben Stoltzfus laid the new pipes into the septic tank. Herman helped put on the new porch floor.

On September 5, 2000 I began a new retirement job at Provident Bookstores. My job was in receiving under the supervision of Gary Herr. It was an excellent three day a week job for me. It was a bit more challenging and better pay than NAPA. I worked there during the transition from Provident Bookstore to Berea in the fall of 2006. By December of 2008 Berea had no more work for me so I was without a job. I checked at various places for a job and found none. So by the end of April 2009 I was back at NAPA.

My last years at NAPA, from 2009 through 2016 were among my best years there. My three supervisors, Steve Headlee, Joe Denver and Stacy Osborn were very capable and our customers seemed happy and satisfied with our services. For most of those years I got to make at least one trip a week to a large NAPA warehouse in Middletown, Delaware. It was a nice approximately 100 mile round trip drive that I enjoyed. For several years I went twice a week. Someone from Gap NAPA went everyday Monday through Friday. But I also enjoyed making local trips mostly within a 15 mile radius of Gap. I considered many of the people to whom we delivered as friends.

Of course all things come to an end. I decided not to drive another winter. I had a few minor accidents on ice and snow so felt it was time for me to quit. For my next retirement job I decided to write my memoirs. And that's what I'm doing now, 2017. Sara and I did some traveling during my retirement and I'll write about that separately. I assume it will be more interesting than this chapter. Or maybe not, I haven't written it yet.

CHAPTER 17

Three Trips to Europe

Sara and I made three trips to Europe after I retired in 1995. Chapter 17 is an account of these trips.

GREECE 2004

After I retired I had occasional invitations to join some ex-Paxers and revisit Greece. For financial and other reasons I always declined. And mostly because of finances I did not join Sophie's Group. However Orville Schmidt kept calling me saying he would like to interview me in Greece about my time in Greece. And he wants to do it while Sophie's Group is there. Sophie was a Greek girl from Tsakones who married a Pax man Gerald or Shorty Jantzi from Nebraska. And Sophie was now leading a tour of Greece for ex-Paxers and friends, a group of 46 people for 15 days. I checked into the possibility of a shorter tour of flying to Athens, renting a car and joining Sophie's Group in Tsakones and Panayitsa and decided to do it along with Sara and Irene. Irene would pay her own expenses.

So on Thursday, September 23, Sara, Irene and I left Kennedy Airport at 6:10 pm and arrived in Athens at 10:30 local time but our luggage didn't. We were informed our luggage should arrive on Saturday so on Friday we drove to Corinth in our rented Hyundai. We toured Corinth on our own and had a very enjoyable evening meal there on a narrow street and a small restaurant. On Saturday at 12:00 we received a call informing us our luggage arrived. We picked it up at the airport and headed for Tsakones in northern Greece. We had a very nice drive through Larissa, Katerini and Berea. We bypassed Edessa and went from Skydra to Aridea. There was a heavy thunder storm in northern Greece on Saturday just before we arrived and knocked out all electricity which we were not aware of. It was evening and got dark soon after Skydra and no electric lights along the way. However I did not think much of it as 50 years ago when I traveled this road there were no lights either. But when we arrived in Aridea it was obvious there was a blackout and we were informed what happened. I saw nothing familiar in Aridea and people were around with make shift lighting. With my very limited Greek I asked. the way the way to Tsakones and we found the way. We had planned to meet Sophie's Group on Saturday pm at a Coffee Shop owned by her brother Costus. But now everything was dark, we saw nobody anywhere and I recognized nothing. Because we saw the sign we knew this was Tsakones or as the sign read TSAKOI. In the dark we drove out of town toward Policarpi and I knew it was wrong so turned around and found our way to Rothinia. There we saw an elderly couple sitting on their porch in candle light. We knew Sophie's Group was planning to stay in a hotel in Loutraki but had no name or address for the hotel. We asked this couple in my broken Greek how to get to Loutraki. They told us to cross the bridge and turn left on the first road which we did. However it was a gravel road and eventually a dirt field lane. Irene was driving. We came by a building where some men were sitting in the dark. We asked them the way to Loutraki. It was complicated and one of the men finally said, "Pomi," and told us to follow him on his bicycle which we did for 10 or 15 minutes. We came to a paved road in Piperia that we were told led to Loutraki. We gave our friend a candy bar and several Euros and headed for Loutraki. We stopped several times when we saw people with makeshift lights and asked for a hotel in Loutraki and they wanted to know which one. Of course we didn't know and while praying kept on going. In the dark I saw the name Filoxenia on a hotel, recognized it meant "friend of foreigners" or something like that and decided to stop. I asked the man at the desk in Greek whether he speaks English. He said, "No, but follow me" in Greek. So I did and there was Sophie's Group in some darkness waiting for supper. Wow! In about 15 minutes after having greeted many people in candle light, the lights went on. We had supper with them. Sara, Irene and I then went to a nearby hotel where Orville Schmidt and Jim Bixler were staying.

On Sunday many of us Americans were at the church in Tsakones, the only place recognizable from 50 years ago. Tsakones now had all paved roads, electricity, television and all new homes usually of brick or marble. Almost unbelievable! It was great to meet Sophie's Group and we toured with them on Sunday after-noon and Monday. On Sunday Sara, Irene and I along with Shorty Jantzi, Ray and Brenda Dyck and Jim Bixler went with Orville in a van and followed Sophie's Group in their bus to Panayitsa. On the way we stopped at Berea where Paul preached and at the tombs of Philip I and II from the 4th century BC. It was great to see Panay-itsa again. Panayitsa had not changed much as Tsakones did. Many homes were built of stone and still there. The Pax house on the outside looked much as it had 50 years ago. The tour group went to a mountain top retreat center especially for the mayor but open to the public. The mayor had a message for us there translated by Sophie. From this spot we could see the lake where Paxers Simon and Eli Miller drowned while swimming in 1954.

On Monday Sophie's Group went to Mt. Athos and had room on the bus so Sara, Irene and I joined them. We all got on a cruise boat at Ouranoupoli and saw the monasteries from the boat. I sat with Luke Martin on the cruise. He, his wife Mary and daughter Rebecca came to Greece on their own as we did. Norman

Kennel and I especially reminisced as we had spent several days together walking on this peninsula along with Arlin Hunsberger and
Dick Lambright in 1957 while in Pax.

I greatly enjoyed being with the tour but the highlight of my
trip was probably on Tuesday and Wednesday. On Tuesday morning Sara, Irene and I drove from our Hotel Asters where we stayed
in or near Loutraki to the coffee shop in Tsakones. For about an
hour we had coffee and talked with Gabriel Findekeedes and others.
I showed them some old pictures I had along. Gabriel then gave us
a mostly walking tour of Tsakones and Rothonia. I saw the fields we
had rented and I had worked in for two years now grown up in trees
and an orchard. Gabriel showed us what had been Grandpa's property, the Pax unit home for about seven years and my home for two
years. There were now no buildings, only rather tall weeds. I literally
had tears when I saw that spot. It was an emotional experience for
me. We saw where the cannery had been in Rothonia. It is now in
a new building. We visited Stalies, our tractor driver, and his wife
made a meal for us. While there Andreas whom I well remembered
came and chatted as did Ken King's mother-in-law. We visited Fotie's
widow nearby. Fotie had been a good friend and great supporters of
the Pax boys. In the evening we joined the tour group for supper
at Toula's house, about 50 of us. Toula is Fotie's daughter, Sophie's
cousin and was the tour guide for Sophie's Group in Greece.

Wednesday morning over breakfast at Hotel Asteras we visited with Vivi, Alex Mavride's daughter. She had been with the tour
since Saturday. Sara, Irene and I then picked up Luke and Mary
Martin at their nearby hotel and drove to Vaso Karipidou's home.
Vaso was expecting us. She had been an MCC Trainee at Luke
Bomberger's home in New Holland Pa in 1962 and visited my
home in Buena Vista. Now at Vaso's home Jim Bixler recorded interviews Orville Schmidt had with Luke Martin and me separately.
I never got to see the finished video.

Late afternoon on Wednesday Luke and Mary Martin joined
Irene, Sara and me for our three day trip to Athens. Our first stop
of interest was Kalambaka where the world famous monasteries of
Meteora are nearby. Irene was driving on a busy street in Kalambaka when she said, "There's Dawn Ranck"! Irene pulled up on the
sidewalk, parked and got Dawn's attention. Dawn was on a tour
tracing the steps of the Apostle Paul. Thursday forenoon we had a
great time visiting two of the monasteries going up and down many
steps and being introduced to history of the ages and had some
wonderful vistas. The six monasteries still occupied I think were
built in the 14th century.

From Meteora we drove over the mountains to Delphi and
had several hours before dark to tour Delphi. Delphi is a quaint
small town and nearby are what remains of a culture that was thriv-
ing in the fifth century BC. It is the best preserved amphitheater
from BC in Greece and maybe in the world. We found a place to
sleep about twenty-five kms from Delphi in another quaint town,
Arachova, in an old hotel on Main Street. On Friday we drove to
Athens and after much difficulty found a hotel not far from the
airport that we could afford for Irene, Sara and me then one down
town for Luke and Mary.

From Luke and Mary's hotel we had a very interesting walk
to the Acropolis. We toured the Acropolis on our own with a printed guide. On Mar's Hill the five of us found a spot to be alone and
Luke read two verses of Acts 17 from his Greek New Testament and
I read the whole chapter from the NRSV. After the Acropolis we
did some gift shopping then found a very nice place to eat outside.
Irene, Sara and I said good-bye to Luke and Mary and went to our
hotel. Saturday morning early we turned in our car and were taken
to the airport. Around 7:00 we left for Paris on Air France. We
spent several hours at the Paris Airport, got some coffee, etc., spent
our last Euros then boarded our same plane, headed across France

and the Atlantic Ocean and landed at Kennedy Airport in New York. Mike was there to greet us and brought us home.

I know this section like some others I wrote is too long and detailed. I'm sorry for those few of you who read it. But I relive much of it as I write which is fun.

CAMINO DE SANTIAGO

Pilgrims were walking on the Camino de Santiago in Spain more than 1,000 years ago. In contrast the Appalachian Trail did not exist 100 years ago. And they are different. The Appalachian Trail goes over mountains through state and national forests far from towns and villages and mostly away from civilization. The Camino on the other hand while also having some mountains goes through every town and village along the way. You can stop at several cafes almost every day to relax, drink coffee and get a bite to eat. And in town you will find an inexpensive place to sleep in your sleeping bag with many other pilgrims. You can walk in a relaxed manner not trying to walk faster or farther than anyone else. And you meet other pilgrims from various countries and languages, mostly European and mostly Catholic. The landscape varies with vineyards, farmland, mountains, sheep and cattle, stone fences, small old quaint villages and markets in larger towns and old cities with a BC date of origin. Pilgrims are on bicycles as well as walking always in the same direction, to Santiago.

The Camino de Santiago was very popular in the 10th through 13th centuries as pilgrims paid homage to the Apostle James where his body lay in a tomb in northwestern Spain. According to tradition and legend after the crucifixion of Jesus the Apostle James went to Spain for a brief time to spread the Gospel but only had seven converts. When he was beheaded in Jerusalem by Herod Agrippa around 44 AD a few of his friends managed to get his body, put it on a boat and miraculously got to Spain where they buried the body. For several centuries it was mostly forgotten that he was buried there but in 813 a Christian hermit discovered the tomb and Santiago, St. James, soon became the patron saint of Spain. Many miracles happened as pilgrims visited his grave. For three or more centuries people from all over Europe made a pilgrimage to honor St. James. Among the more notable pilgrims were Charlemagne, St. Francis of Assisi and King Ferdinand and Queen Isabella of Spain. After the Protestant Reformation of the 16th century, pilgrimages to Santiago declined significantly and kept declining. By the 20th century very few pilgrims walked the Camino anymore. In the late 1960s a guidebook was published and by 1980 the Camino was again becoming popular, now for modern pilgrims. In 1982 Pope John Paul II became the first pontiff to visit Santiago.

I was interested in the Camino de Santiago because Sara could be along and enjoy it even though she could not walk it. Also I had this idea of every five years doing a major hike and I had never been to Spain! Although our financial situation wasn't the greatest we had more than enough to walk a portion of the Trail and the children said, "Do it!" So in 2005 I fulfilled my dream of walking the Camino de Santiago as a pilgrim mostly, not a tourist, although I was both.

When Arno Thimm from Holland found out I wanted to walk the Camino he said he wanted to walk with me. So we decided that Sara and I would fly to Amsterdam and we would go together. However Jacqueline, Arno's wife, developed cancer and Arno decided not to go. But our two youngest children, Irene and Herman, both decided to take vacation and join us. Their decision was made partially because they felt Sara and I could not do it alone but they also both wanted the experience. Herman was taking a year off from teaching so time off was no problem. Irene had limited vacation so she met us in Spain and left from Spain.

On September 7 Sara, Herman and I flew from Newark, NJ to Amsterdam, spent a day with Arno and Jacqueline Thimm in Haarlem, rented an Opel and headed for Spain. We especially enjoyed the scenery south of Paris. Much less traffic, lots of sheep, various kinds of cows, many vineyards and before entering Spain the Pyrenees Mountains. Our first destination in Spain was Burgos. I had some contacts with missionary Dennis Byler and we visited him in his home in a village not far from Burgos. His wife Connie was in Bolivia with her father who was not well. On Sunday we worshiped at the Mennonite Church in Burgos where Dennis preached but he is not the pastor. Everything was in Spanish of course. Several of the people who could speak English helped us understand much of what was happening and being said. We declined an invitation to go home with a family because we wanted to meet Irene at the train station in Leon at 4:00, a two hour drive.

We did meet Irene as planned and found a hotel to stay for the night. Early Monday morning Herman and I got on the Camino in Leon and headed for Santiago a little under 200 miles away. Because of not being marked well we got on the wrong trail soon after Leon and needed to walk back. Two men from Germany, a lady from Australia and one from New Zealand had also just started the Camino at Leon, made the same error we did and walked back with us. We somewhat kept in touch with the German men and one of them, Wolfgang, finished with us. I only walked several hours when I began getting blisters on my toes. By evening my blisters were serious. Sara and Irene met Herman and me that evening but did not stay with us. However Irene went to a Pharmacy and did what she could to take care of my blisters. The next morning when I was putting on my shoes I discovered I had put an extra shoe lace in each shoe at home and that was the reason for my blisters. My feet really hurt while walking and the third day on the Camino in the mountains a young boy was there selling canes and

I bought two of them for 5.00 Euros each. They helped considerably.

Before leaving home I read how people take a prayer stone from their garden and place it at a large pole on the Camino. I took a prayer stone along and with thousands of others through the centuries placed a stone at the pole on the fourth day of our pilgrimage. On the evening of that same day the four of us had a hotel room together and went out for early dinner. We discovered restaurants are open noon to 5:00 then 7:00-11:00, also for breakfast. So we waited till 7:00. Our German friends, Christian and Wolfgang were there and a lady pilgrim from Germany so we got a table together and that was our table for the evening. The meal came in three servings and wine was a part of it. It was a different experience for us. Sara and I did not drink wine but everyone else did.

Every hostel was different and interesting. Hostels were only for people who were walking and had no access to a vehicle. Some charged 5.00-7.00 Euros while others were by donations only. Often there were 30-80 or more beds in a room generally with no covers. A very interesting and smaller one was run by two Catholic brothers whom Herman and I got to know rather well. About every third or fourth night the four of us had a hotel room together.

I did not get to know anyone real well on the trail but did have long conversations with some. One was a man from Rhode Island, a Catholic walking as a pilgrim. We probably chatted for an hour and were delighted to discover that Henri Nouwen was a mentor for both of us. I think we saw Wolfgang, one of the German men we had dinner with, every day. He started and finished the Camino when we did but we seldom walked together. However he often was a help to us in finding a place to eat or stay in the evening as he could speak Spanish and some English. Also I could communicate with him fairly well in German. I had some long conversations with Karlene, a Methodist lady from Iowa and her friend Jean from Hawaii. I had several e-mail communications with Karlene after I was home. And we walked with a group of mostly women Catholics from Germany several days before Santiago and got to know each other fairly well.

In total I was on the Camino 13 days, sometimes with Irene, sometimes with Herman and sometimes with both of them. No two days were alike, sometimes through vineyards, sometimes over mountains, some days stone fences on either side of the trail, almost every day through an old village with a cafe and occasionally through towns and cities. I had a copy of "The Pilgrim Prayer" by Tom Peffer and Joyce Rupp with me that I prayed in the morning:

> *Guardian of my soul,*
> *guide me on my way this day.*
> *Keep me safe from harm.*
> *Deepen my relationship with you,*
> *your Earth, and all your family.*
> *Strengthen your love within me*
> *that I may be a presence of your peace in our world*
> *Amen.*

For five years I wondered and dreamed what Santiago might be like. Now on Saturday forenoon, September 24, 2005 while walking on the Camino, I saw the sign indicating Santiago city limits and I was walking into it. I could hardly believe it was happening but it was! The Camino went through narrow streets to the large Santiago Cathedral de Compostela where the Apostle James is buried. We had some time before the 12:00 mass and took a few pictures from the large plaza. In the cathedral Sara and I got to walk down the steps and go by the urn or coffin of the Apostle James. We then found a seat near the front of the sanctuary with our German lady Catholic pilgrim friends. The large Cathedral sanctuary filled with people and mass lasted about an hour. An especially interesting part of the service was the large "Holy Blessing Vessel" on long, long ropes swinging up and down. It took sixty years to build the large cathedral, 1075-1135. After mass I guess I was no longer a pilgrim on a pilgrimage but a tourist. Being a tourist was also interesting.

Many pilgrims take the Camino Finisterre and walk to Finisterre, the End of the World at the Atlantic Ocean an approximate 50 mile trail. We had hoped to drive there but Irene needed to be in Madrid to get her flight home so we headed for Madrid. Because it was not out of our way we drove through northeastern Portugal for about 100 miles mostly on secondary, very hilly and mountainous roads, which we enjoyed. We left Irene at Madrid and Sara, Herman and I headed for Bienenberg in Switzerland. Toll roads in Spain and France were very expensive so we took some secondary roads. Our first night without Irene was in the Pyrenees near the French border, very scenic. Had a great drive through Lyons in France, Geneva, the Rhone River and Jura Mountains in Switzerland—no toll roads in Switzerland anywhere, at least we didn't have any. We arrived in Bienenberg by Liestal on Tuesday evening September 27. We had hoped to get an overnight room in Bienenberg but there was a Boot Camp group there for the week and there was no room in the Inn for us. They got a room for us in nearby Pratteln.

On Wednesday we drove to Zurich and saw some things of Anabaptist history like the Grossmünster Kirche and the plaque along the Limmat River giving the story of the drowning of Felix Manz. In Zurich was the first we saw someone carrying a coffee cup while walking since leaving Holland. In Spain you sit and relax to enjoy your food and drink. We had our evening meal at Bienenberg. While at our table eating a girl from the Boot Camp group came by and asked where we were from. Here it was Anna Landes from Lititz, PA and she works at Provident Bookstore in Ephrata, I was working at Provident Bookstore in Lancaster and we had been at some meetings together. On Thursday morning we came back to Bienenberg for a tour arranged by Irma Rifenacht for Sara and me but led by Rosemarie Wälti who could speak English. I enjoyed the tour very much as this is where I was in Bible School for three months in 1957-1958. After the tour we went to the Eldersheim in Muttenz by Liestal and had our noon meal with Samuel and Irma Gerber as pre-arranged. Lisel Widmer, now 89 and nearly blind, whom I knew 50 years ago, joined us. Samuel was one of my teachers at Bienenberg Bible School when I was there. He and Irma visited us at our home in Buena Vista near Gap a time or two.

From the Eldersheim in Liestal Sara, Herman and I drove through the Schwarzwald or Black Forest in Germany to Wissenbourg, France, where Werner Hirschler met us at the Autobahn exit. Werner took us to his home in the dorf of Geisberg. Werner's wife is Martha Oesch from Luxembourg and they were both in Bienenberg Bible School when I was. Martha was also an MCC Trainee in the David and Rhoda King home for six months not far from Gap, PA. Werner and Martha were great hosts for us. While in Wissembourg we had lunch at Theo and Suzanne Hege's home. Theo comes from a large family and his sister Erica is married to Frank Shirk, a Mennonite bishop, and lives in Leola, Pa. Theo was also a student at Bienenberg Bible School when I was. Theo gave us a tour of Schaffsbusch, the large Hege farm.

Because I am a descendant of Nicholas Stoltzfus we drove to nearby Zweibrücken and visited the farm where Nicholas worked and lived just prior to migrating to America. In Zweibrücken we met Werner and Irmtraud Schowalter who took us in their car to Ringweilerhof, the former home of Nicholas. We were impressed how the many buildings were kept in very good shape. Mennonites by the name of Schowalter operate the farm now. They were not home but their daughter treated us to coffee and scrumptious cookies. We also visited a nearby mill at Hornbach where Nicholas worked at one time. At Zweibrücken we saw what was an Amish House of Prayer or a place to worship and also the current Mennonite Church where Arno Thimm was pastor at one time. We have a good friend back home, Fred Gascho, who is from Zweibrücken.

After Wissenbourg, France, we drove to Enkenbach, Germany where I was in Pax service in 1955. We found Weichselstrasse, the street along which we built ten or so houses and lived in one of them. We met a Mennonite lady who got me acclimated a bit then introduced us to Rainer and Roswitha Schmidt. Rainer was a young boy living in the Siedlung when I was there and remembers us Pax boys very well. He and his wife now live in what was the Pax Unit house where I lived. They treated us royally and gave us a meal. They did not have room to keep us overnight. He wrote a personal note of thanks to me for helping build the homes on Weichselstrasse. Our overnight hosts were Andres and Jolene Wehner. Jolene was formerly from Lancaster Country, PA. On Sunday we attended the Enkenbach Mennonite Church. An addition has been added to what the Pax boys built. At church they had a brief memorial service for Ericka Thimm who had cancer. She was married to Arno Thimm's brother Egon whom we had briefly visited on Saturday. We also met Amanda Shank who was an exchange student here from Lancaster Mennonite High School and a daughter of Roland Shank Jr.

Sunday afternoon we drove from Enkenbach Germany to Haarlem in the Netherlands, a distance of 500 kms or 300 miles. We arrived at Arno and Jacqueline Thimm's home at 6:30. On Monday morning we took our Opel back to Avis. We put on 7,300 kms and it cost us 860 Euros. Arno gave us a tour of the Mennonite Church he pastored for almost 20 years, a hidden church with

*On our way to the Camino de Santiago we got our rental car at Haarlem and
Sara and I had a wonderful time with Arno and Jacqueline Thimm in their
home. Herman is with us and Irene will join us in Spain.*

*Because of blisters on my feet I bought two canes from a boy along the trail to help
me walk to Santiago. Irene is with me.*

Eventually the trail will lead to a farm village or a small town with a cafe but mostly it is open country.

There are many of these corn crib like structures along the trail and I'm not sure what they are.

The Camino is for people on bicycles and horse back riders as well as walking but not always together.

Sara, Irene and I are observing many old buildings in Santiago as we near the plaza and the cathedral.

It took 60 years to build the Santiago Cathedral de Compostela, completed in 1135, where St. James is believed to be buried. The Cathedral is the end of the Camino.

On our way back to Haarlem, Sara and I stopped at Bienenberg where I attended European Mennonite Bible School in 1957-1958.

We also stopped at Enkenbach, Germany. Here Rainer Schmidt and I are looking at houses built by Pax boys.

Sara and I are enjoying a delicious meal with Rainer and Roswitha Schmidt in their home. It is the house I lived in when I was a Pax boy in 1955. The unattended plate is Herman's.

Sara and Omar at the Iquazu Falls in Brazil while attending MWC in Paraguay.

Sara and Omar at Machu Picchu in Peru while attending MWC in Paraguay.

On Mars Hill in Athens in 2004. Mary Martin, Luke Martin, Omar, Sara, Irene. Luke read two verses of Acts 17 from his Greek New Testament and I read the whole chapter in English.

no street entrance. It was built in 1683 and currently has a thousand members. On Tuesday Arno and Jacqueline took Sara and me to Pengjun in Friesland where we met Tineka Nauta. Tineka was at workcamp in Elixhausen by Salzburg with me in 1957. Tineka went with us to Witmarsum where we saw the Menno Simons Memorial. We had a picnic on the big dike that separates the North Sea from Usselmeer which is fresh water. Then we drove on the 30 km long dike to get to Freisland and back. The chief engineer of the dike was a Mennonite.

On Wednesday back at Haarlem Sara and I had a very interesting one and a half hour tour of the Hiding Place, Corrie Ten Boom's home. We also went to Amsterdam on the train with Arno and had a one hour boat ride tour of Amsterdam. On Thursday we said good-bye to Arno and Jacqueline who had been very gracious hosts. We got on the plane at Amsterdam at 1:30 with the two walking canes I bought on the Camino de Santiago. Arrived at Newark at 4:20 and Sherilyn and her sister Jeanette were there and brought us home. Herman bought a new bicycle in Haarlem and is touring Holland for a week before he comes home.

This ends my Camino de Santiago Pilgrimage.

HERITAGE TOUR, PASSION PLAY

In the summer of 2010, July16-August 2, Sara and I joined a group of 31 people led by Lemar and Lois Ann Mast for a heritage tour in Europe, mostly Germany, France and Switzerland. We flew Air India Newark NJ to Frankfurt, Germany. Our first stop was Mainz where we toured the Gutenberg Museum and also enjoyed the nearby outdoor market. Sara and I were surprised a cup of coffee, no refills, cost 4.00 Euros, almost $5.00. From Mainz we had a scenic drive with hair pin curves to Boppard on the Rhine on our bus. On Sunday we had a four and a half hour boat ride on the Rhine from Boppard to Bingen, vineyards and castles all along the way. It was special to see the famous legendary Lorelei Rock again. One of our group read an English translation of the Lorelei poem as we went by.

Our tour bus picked us up at Bingen. On our way to Strasbourg, France we visited Ringweilerhof by Zweibrücken where my ancestor Nicholas Stoltzfus was hired man several years before he left for America in 1766. In Strasbourg two highlights were eating outside along a canal and touring the huge Gothic Strasbourg Cathedral built 1176-1439. The Cathedral was designed to have two towers but the second tower was never constructed.

Because of severe persecution in Switzerland many Anabaptist, including Amish, fled to southern France in the 1700s. During this time in the area of Markich, now Ste Marie-aux-Mines, seventy percent of the farms were Amish. Jacob Ammann lived here in his later years. It reminded me a bit of parts of Lancaster County PA and Holmes County OH today where probably seventy percent of the farms are Amish. Our first stop after Strasbourg was the home of Amish Elder Nicholas Augspurger, 1801-1890. Elder Augspurger was known for his knowledge of herbs and medicinal plants to cure diseases for both humans and animals. Some stories written about him at that time are still available so we probably have more knowledge about him than any other Amish person of his time. His home is still in good shape. It has a large room where the Amish had worship services. An Amish graveyard is nearby. We spent considerable time at the Ohnenheim Mill not far away which we think is the mill where the Swiss, German and French Anabaptist signed the Dortrecht Confession of Faith in 1693, earlier signed by the Dutch. Jacob Ammann refused to sign it. He was okay with the Schleitheim Confession but did not agree with the Dortrecht. Ammann had many followers in this part of Alsace. The mill we visited was built in 1469. There is some evidence this may be the mill of the historic occasion but not one hundred percent evidence at this point.

After the Ohnenheim Mill we had a brief tour of Unter Linden Museum in Colmar. As we entered Colmar we saw a Statue of Liberty replica as the sculptor of the Statue in New York harbor is from Colmar. We then drove some distance and spent considerable time in a large open museum displaying life from 1850-1950. I found it very interesting. Lots of storks and stork nests. Our hotel for the next three days was on the outskirts of Montbelaird and we discovered it was built on the former farm of a Roth ancestor of Marian Stoltzfus. Marian is with our tour group. Some local Mennonites had the evening meal with us at our hotel. I showed them pictures, names and addresses of young people who were at Bienenberg Bible School in 1957-1958 when I was and they knew many of them. One of the local men, a historian, has been to Lancaster County and knew two of my Amish neighbors, Ben Blank and Abner Beiler, also historians.

From Montbeliard we visited three local Mennonite churches and their graveyards. In the graveyard of our first church I saw the following names: Moser, Yoder, Graber, Zaugg, Hirschy, Klopstein, Rediger, Roth (Marian's ancestors), Geiser, Widmer and Amstutz. The second church, Birkenhof, has 140 members. We met the historian, Jean Pierrer Nussbaumer, who was at Peter Dyck's memorial service in Akron PA where Sara and I were also. Our third church was almost in Montbeliard and is the largest Mennonite Church in France, 220 members. They also have the oldest Mennonite Church record book in the world begun only in 1770 but recorded many prior records. Anabaptists did not keep record books because they could be a source of execution if your name was found. We also had a tour of the town Montbeliard and were informed that a large old stone bench near the market was a meeting place for the Mennonites and Amish. This is Jacob Ammann country. Most of my ancestors when persecuted in Switzerland went to the Pfalz or Palatinate in Germany rather than to Alsace in France.

We also toured the Peugeot Museum with 120 cars on display from 1891-2008 plus bicycles, trucks and smaller items.

It rained when we entered Switzerland after Montbeliard so we toured Bern from the bus while driving through the city. Lois Ann pointed out the Aare River where many Anabaptist were put on boats, exiled and never heard of again. From Bern we went through Burgdorf and then an unbelievable pretty mountainous drive to Affoltern where a Mennonite family has the Emmantaler Schaukäserai AG, a large cheese factory. We saw them make cheese both the present modern way and the old fashioned way. From there we had another wonderful trip through the mountains through Wasen to Lüdernalp. We got our first sight of the snow capped Alps in the distance. Also three men with Alpine horns gave us a concert. There was a bus load of Conservative Mennonites also staying at our hotel with Lewis Overholt and the Golden Rule Tour. One of them, Vada Unruh from Linden, Alberta, was familiar with the concrete business of Peter and Donna Remple. Donna is my niece.

Our five days in Switzerland were very informative and enjoyable. After the cheese factory our first stop was at the Hans Haslibacher Hof. Hans was the last Anabaptist to be executed in the Bern area. He was beheaded in 1581 and had a conversation with an angel just before execution. The last hymn in the Ausbund is about him. The hymn has thirty-two verses and several of these verses are still occasionally selected to be sung at Amish worship services. Sara signed the guest book here at the Hof and was surprised and delighted to see Elmer and Susie Lapp's names from Coatesville, PA entered very recently. Elmer is my nephew and he and Susie had recently toured Switzerland with four other Amish couples. After the Haslibacher Hof we toured the nearby Trachselwald Castle built in 1220. Here many Anabaptists were imprisoned. They were pulled up to a second floor window and that was their only way of escape. Steps on the inside have now been built and we could walk up. Hans Haslibacher was imprisoned here before he was executed. In Langnau several miles south of Trachselwald we visited the oldest Mennonite Church in the world. The Emmental Church was built in 1571 as a hidden Church, part of a house, which it still is. The nearby cemetery has familiar Mennonite names. I bought a cowbell at Langnau for about $15.00 that I still have.

On Sunday our group worshiped at the Reformed Church in Guggisberg. We all had lunch there but needed to pay about $24.00 each which I thought was too much. Nearby we stopped where the Jacob Hochstetler family lived at one time before migrating to America in 1736. Twenty-one years after being in America and living in the Amish community along Northkill Creek in Berks County PA Jacob and two younger sons were taken captive by Indians while the mother and two children were killed. Sara is a descendant of three of Jacob's children. In Switzerland a Brenneman family now lives where the Hochstetlers lived and they showed us a "hiding place" in the barn where Anabaptists could briefly hide while trying to escape.

Sunday afternoon we drove to Erlenbach where Jacob Ammann was born and baptized. The house where Jacob was born is up in the Alps about a mile from Erlenbach along a very narrow road and our group needed to walk the last quarter mile. Jacob's father was a tailor and Jacob became a tailor as well. Jacob was baptized as a baby in 1642 in the Reformed Church in Erlenbach. Jacob left Erlenbach as a young man and went to Thun possibly to get a job. We don't know when he was rebaptized as an adult. He was in prison at one time for being Anabaptist. It's not known when he went to Alsace but he was living there when the signing of the Dortrect Confession of Faith took place at Ohnenheim Mill in 1693. Jacob was among those who did not sign it.

Before our tour group left home everyone had to decide whether they wanted reservations to take a train to the top of the mountain Jungfrau. If the weather is nice it's a great experience but many days the mountain is in clouds with no view from the top. Twenty-three of our group of thirty-one decided to take the risk. It was worth it even though we were in the clouds much of the time at the top. Those of us who went walked to the train station at Lauterbrunnen from our hotel carrying our breakfast in paper bags. Although it was cloudy we had a great view most of the time to Kleine Sheidegg about halfway to the top. The second train was mostly tunnels and at the top we were in a cloud. One of the many things to do at the top besides eat, buy gifts and look out at the clouds was the Ice Palace with many rooms and passage ways and many great ice carvings inside a glacier. It was rather awesome. The clouds partially lifted at times and we had a great view of the glacier but not the valley. But we had a nice ride going down from Jungfraujoch after we were out of the clouds.

Once on our bus again we had an enjoyable drive through Interlaken then along the Brienzer See to Brienz and our hotel. Brienz was established in 1146. Sara and I had a real surprise when we were given a special place at the table and a big cake with our names and "47 Wedding Anniversary" on it. We had to cut the first two pieces of cake then the cake was shared with everyone. About a dozen men yodelers were part of the evening entertainment. I have no pictures of this from my camera because that evening I deleted all my pictures in error that I had taken thus far. The next day July 27 was actually our anniversary day so Sara and I celebrated by eating ice cream while we were in Luzern by the lake and the famous covered footbridge. From Luzern we drove to Hirzel where Johanna Spyri, author of Heidi, lived and wrote her books. It's a wonderful view of the Alps from her home. Near there we saw where Hans Landis lived. Hans was the last Anabaptist to be executed in Zurich. We then got an interesting hotel in Kappel near Zurich that was built as a large Nunnery, now a Reformed Retreat Center and looks like a monastery. Conrad Grebel and Ulrich Zwingly met in this building for discussions about Scripture. There is a Zwingly Monument up the road a bit which I walked to. I think Zwingly died in a battle here.

We had a full day Wednesday as we visited Zurich, Zolliken and Täuferhöhle by Baretswil. Peter Detweiler, a Reformed pastor who initiated the then recent reconciliation between the Reformed and the Anabaptist, was our guide for most of the day. Several from our group put on a very meaningful drama just outside of Felix Manz's house where Conrad Grebel, Feliz Manz and George Blaurock baptized each other as adults on January 21, 1525. They were the first to openly break away from Ulrich Zwingly. Felix was imprisoned then drowned in the nearby Limmat River in January 1527. Between 1527 and 1532 five other Anabaptist were drowned here. For 300 years there was no place for Catholics, Jews, or Anabaptists in Zurich, only Reformed. From Zurich we drove to nearby Zolliken where the newly baptized adults first met secretly for worship. George Blaurock was pastor of the Reformed Church there but resigned.

Täuferhöhle is a large hidden cave where Anabaptist met in secret to worship and pray. Some baptisms and weddings were performed here. It was raining lightly when our bus parked and gave opportunity for whoever so desired to walk a half mile up a narrow, rocky, hilly path to the cave. James Mast, who had been there on previous visits, gave Sara and me his umbrella so we could go while he stayed on the bus. For Sara it was a very difficult walk but we made it. Sue Steffy and others led in a time of prayer and worship. After some of the group left Russ Smucker and I shared a footwashing with water from the Limmat in Zurich that Bernadine Mast had carried up. It was an emotional experience for me.

On Thursday morning we had our breakfast as usual in the basement of the interesting Convent at Kappel where we stayed then had a beautiful drive through the Alps to Innsbruck, Austria. On the way we stopped in the small country of Liechtenstein for lunch and to spend our last Swiss francs as Swiss francs can't be changed to Euros. Switzerland has its own money and does not use Euros as all the surrounding countries do. At Innsbruck we stayed in Hotel Goldene Krone a block from an old tower where Hans Hut, the apostle for the Anabaptist in Austria, was imprisoned.

Our next stop was a five star hotel in Bad Kohlgrub near Oberammergau in Bavaria, Germany. In Oberammergau we saw the 41st performance of the Passion Play. The origin of the Passion Play goes back to 1633 when the residents of Oberammergau vowed if God spared them from bubonic plague ravaging the region they would produce a play depicting the life and death of Jesus that would continue for all time. The villagers believed their prayers were answered and kept their part of the vow when the play was first performed in 1634. The play is always performed during the year ending in zero for five months. The production involves over 2,000 performers, musicians, stage technicians and all are residents of the village. It was partially because of the Passion Play that Sara and I decided to take the Heritage Tour of 2010. The Play was magnificent of course and very dramatic. It is given in German and we each had the printed text in both German and English. Although I know German somewhat I could not understand it very well. When I tried to follow the English script I often lost my place. However I got much of the message, it did effect me and I was glad to have participated by observing. Before the Play Sara and I were surprised to see and get acquainted with a New Order Amish couple in a nearby store, Jerry and Amanda Schlabach from Holmes County, Ohio. Sara knew who they were and we chatted a while.

Saturday we spent several hours at Dachau, a former concentration camp north of Munich where there were over 40,000 deaths between 1933-1945, mostly Jews. It was not a pleasant experience to view the pictures and videos of the happenings there. Our next stop was Triberg in the Black Forest where we stayed for the night. Triberg is known for its spectacular waterfalls and its many cuckoo clocks. Sara and I bought some gifts here as we were nearing the end of our tour but we did not buy a cuckoo clock.

On our trip from Triberg to Worms on Sunday our first stop was at Emmendingen. Emmendingen was special to me because the Königs along with other Anabaptist lived here. I was told my ancestor Samuel König probably lived in Freiburg very near here before coming to America as a 16 year old and would have been here in Emmendingen. In America Samuel married Widow Barbara Yoder's daughter Anna. Samuel and Anna are my ancestors eight ways. Our tour group had a morning worship here outside standing in a circle.

Our next stop was Weinsberg by Heilbron, especially meaningful to Sara because she is from Winesburg, Ohio. The two Weinsbergs are sister cities. And Weinsberg, Germany has an event from the 12th century that is remembered and retold, partially legend but mostly true. A neighboring Duke overtook Weinsberg and the town people fled to their castle on top of the hill for protection. Supposedly the neighboring Duke had planned to kill everybody but one or several women came and pleaded with him to let the women escape with what they could carry and the Duke agreed. So the women carried their husbands on their backs out of the castle. When the Duke saw what was happening he left it go and made a truce. There is now a large statue or memorial in Weinsberg of this event.

Worms was the last stop of our tour. Here in the large Cathedral of St. Peter is where Martin Luther appeared at the Diet of

Worms in 1521 and was accused of heresy resulting from posting his 95 thesis on the church at Wittemberg in 1517. While on trial he said, "Here I stand, I can do no other." or something like that in German. The Luther Monument in Worms is the largest Reformation monument in the world and contains statues of the most important people in the German Reformation including Peter Waldo and John Wycliffe. Luther translated the Bible into German first printed in 1534. Horst Gerlach, a German Mennonite historian, ate with us at our hotel in Worms and spent the evening with us. Our group played social bingo together. Monday morning we had breakfast at 4:00, got on our bus at 4:30 and left by Air India from Frankfurt Airport. Our flight was delayed an hour because a passenger checked in his luggage but did not get on the plane. For those of us going to Masthof at Morgantown the Masthof bus picked us up at Newark and by 3:30 we were at Masthof. A wonderful trip but this is not the end.

A year later, July 29 to July 31, 2011 twenty-one of us who were together for the tour were together again at James and Bernadine Masts at Benton near Millersburg, Ohio and had a wonderful reunion. Had "haystacks" for dinner and everyone shared about recent travels etc. Sara and I went home with John and Sandra Gindlesberger both Friday and Saturday night. On Saturday we all toured Holmes County. On Sunday Russ Smucker led us in our morning worship at the Masts. After a great reunion Sara and I stayed at Uncle Tom's Cabin and visited with Sara's family before driving home on Monday. Uncle Tom is Sara's nephew.

Descendants of Nicholas Stoltzfus standing at the entrance to the farm Nicholas lived near Zweibrücken, Germany. Omar, Marcy Kerstetler, Marian Stoltzfus, Russ Smucker.

Ten descendants of Jacob Hochstetler standing on a farm in Germany where the Hochstetler family lived before migrating to Berks County, Pa.

Omar and Theo Hege on Theo's farm in France. This family of 16 children lost nearly everything during World War II. Theo's sister Erica married Frank Shirk and lives in Lancaster, Pa.

A picture of Erlenbach, Switzerland, taken from Jacob Ammann's home. Jacob is known as the founder of the Amish church.

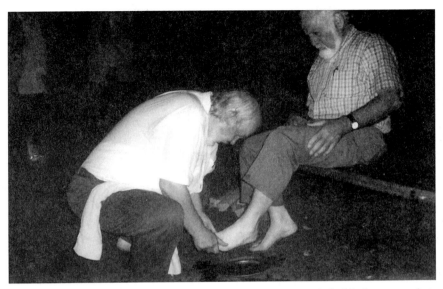

Russ Smucker and I experienced footwashing in the "Täuferhöhle," a cave where early Anabaptists met in secret.

A wonderful Alpine horn concert by Hotel Ludernalp in Switzerland that Sara and I enjoyed on our 2010 Heritage trip.

Sara by the "Weibertreu" monument in Weinsberg, Germany. Sara was born in Winesburg, Ohio, a sister city to Weinsberg, Germany. Read the story concerning the monument in chapter 17.

CHAPTER 18

Alberta and the West Coast

In the fall of 1987 when my brother Seth and his wife Hazel were visiting us I overheard Seth ask Irene our daughter whether she and a friend would drive Seth's car on a trip to visit Donna, their daughter in Alberta, Canada. Irene's answer several weeks later was that she could not do it. I thought that would be a trip Sara and I would really enjoy and Sara agreed. I checked with Provident Bookstore where I worked and got approval that with vacation and times off I could take a five week trip. We informed Seth and Hazel and they were delighted.

Before leaving I made a potential itinerary for the five weeks and rented a pop-up trailer from local friends Paul and Mary Zehr. Sunday afternoon, May 1, 1988 the four of us, Seth , Hazel, Sara and I left Seth and Hazel's home near Myerstown in Seth's Dodge Mitsubishi pulling our pop-up trailer and headed for Alberta, Canada. Our first stop was Port Allegany, PA where my younger brother John and family lived. North of Williamsport, before arriving at Johns, I was driving and fined $80.00 for going over the speed limit, a not so pleasant beginning. We had a nice visit at John and Floy's home.

On Monday we drove north through New York state and went through customs at Buffalo. Had very heavy traffic from Buffalo through Toronto. Then it was sparsely settled and not much traffic. At Sudbury we got on the Trans Canada Highway, route 17 in Ontario, and headed west. Our first two campgrounds in

Canada were not open yet for the season but we managed to stay
anyway. We had a beautiful drive from Sault Ste. Marie to Thunder
Bay with many, many lakes and some mountains. From Thunder
Bay to Dryden was rather forlorn bush country with a few lakes but
almost no population. Saw a sign that informed us that all water
from here flows into the Arctic. Hazel knew Mennonites lived in
the vicinity of Dryden. At McDonald's in Dryden several Indian
girls talked with Hazel and said they attended a Mennonite School
at nearby Beaver Lake and invited us to follow them to the Mennonite community there which we did. The reward was tremendous.
Beaver Lake was beautiful and we found out about Northern Youth
Program started by Clair Schnupp. Jared Yoder from Goshen, Indiana gave us a tour of the headquarters. We discovered he was a
son of Ed and Treva Nissley Yoder from Nappanee, Indiana whom
we knew. And we met Verna Miller Esh, wife of Amos Esh, from
Lancaster Country whom we also knew.

After Dryden we drove through Vermilion Bay which is only
about 120 miles south of Red Lake where a dozen or more of my
friends served in Voluntary Service but I was never there. Manitoba
was a major stop for us because Anna Wenger with whom I worked
at Provident Bookstore was now in Winnipeg in Voluntary Service.
We spent two nights and a day with her. Anna was a great hostess.
She gave us a tour of Steinbach as well as Winnipeg and introduced
us to her special friend Ron Reimer. We saw where Mennonite
World Conference would be held in 1990.

We continued west on Trans-Canada Highway, now route
1, through the prairies of southern Manitoba and Saskatchewan,
a beautiful drive. On Friday night we stayed in a campground
north of Swift Current. Driving through town we saw the large
Zion Mennonite Church. After Swift Current we drove through
Medicine Hat and Taber arriving at Jake and Helen Rempels near
Vauxhall, Alberta, mid-afternoon. Jake and Helen are the parents

of Seth and Hazel's son-in-law Peter Rempel and Peter was there as well as his sister Mary from Lethbridge. On Sunday we attended the Mennonite Brethren Church in Vauxhall with them. It was Mother's Day and the children gave a program of which I remember only the following. While up front one of the children announced aloud within everyone's hearing, "Mommy I'm wet!" Over dinner back at the Rempels we heard Jake and Helen's stories about Russia and World War I as well as Mary's various stories including being held captive by Cannibals for eight days. We arrived at Pete and Donna's home at Warburg, southwest of Edmonton, after dark on Sunday eve. They have a beautiful home right by the North Saskatchewan River. Peter has cattle. We spent a week with Pete and Donna and their three boys, Linford, Mike and Sheldon.

On Tuesday Sara and I took Seth's car and the pop-up trailer for an enjoyable, scenic two day 700 mile trip to Jasper and Banff National Parks. The Canadian Rockies are beautiful! On the Bow River Parkway heading into the town of Banff we saw a lot of deer, elk, and mountain sheep grazing along the road. From the Tunnel Mountain Campground in Banff where we stayed we saw snow capped mountains on both sides of our trailer. In the morning we took a gondola to the top of a mountain and ate breakfast with a great view on all four sides including all of Banff. At noon we had soup and coffee by Lake Louise then back to Pete's, passing a Hutterite Colony along Medicine River.

On Thursday evening we had a tour of a nearby Hutterite Colony. Two girls, Helen and Dorothy Welf, took us on a tour of the colony. We saw their air grain seeder with which they seed about 400 acres in a 16 hour day. They seed approximately 4,000 acres and have seven combines. The girls took us to their homes and we had an enjoyable visit. They sang two songs for us, one in German and one in English.

On Friday Sara and I with Seth's car drove to Athabasca where Patty Prokopchuk's parents, Frank and Dorothy live. Patty is a friend of our daughter Irene and has been in our home several times. While at the Prokopchuks we mentioned Calling Lake. Dorothy said she works there and would be glad to take us there which she did. We knew people from near home had been to Calling Lake as missionaries. At the store in Calling Lake I was shocked and surprised when the proprietor came out and I knew him! It was Willis Amstutz who was at Eastern Mennonite College when I was. He and his wife, Joyce, had been operating the store for many years. We had a nice visit. Sara and I had supper at Frank and Dorothy's home and arrived back at Pete's around 10:00, a trip of 355 miles.

On Saturday we went to the nearby Edmonton West Mall, the largest shopping mall under roof in the world at that time. Seth and Hazel had motorized carts so they didn't need to walk. Among other things we went for a submarine ride and saw a lot of aquatic life including shark, swordfish, lockjaw fish and porpoises. We all had a train ride and some of us went on bumper cars with the boys. Pete was the only one who took the roller coaster ride. After we arrived home at Pete's we played Shanghai until 1:00 am.

On Sunday we went to Uncle Peter Rempel's church in Edmonton. In the afternoon Pete took Sara and me to see Rudy Weibe's house nearby. It is a retreat center where writers and other professionals come for retreats. We saw Rudy on the road leaving as we approached his place. Back at Pete's we packed up and got ready to leave for British Columbia and Oregon.

Monday morning we got up before 5:00, ate breakfast with Pete, Donna and the boys and left soon after 6:00 for Ashcraft, B.C. We had a fantastic trip through the Canadian Rockies, especially Highway One from Banff west. Sometime after lunch at Golden it was raining, our lights were dim and the windshield wipers hardly operated. We found an open garage at Salmon Arm where they took out the alternator, cleaned it and everything worked. We could not find a campground at Ashcroft so we went to the ranch where Pete and Donna had lived for a year. Trevor and Bernice Thibauld invited us in for tea. Trevor is a cowboy for the ranch and had worked with Pete. John Regier and his wife who manage the ranch also visited a while. Seth and Hazel are sleeping in Trevor's bed. Sara and I are in the trailer and can hear the coyotes howl.

Trevor and Bernice had breakfast of pancakes and sausages for us at 5:30 and soon after 6:00 we were on our way to Oregon. We were on the Trans-Canada Highway along the Thompson River and later the Fraser River. The Fraser Valley has green grass and farms, an interesting change from mountains and sage brush. We entered the United States at Abbotsford, BC into Washington and got I5 at Bellingham. In Oregon we took US route 30 west along the Columbia River to Astoria by the Pacific Ocean where route 30 ends or begins. Route 30 goes through Gap, PA near my home. We then drove south to Ecola and stopped at the Christian Retreat Center. We saw the Bible School there where Herman and many others from Pennsylvania attended. We also drove to Ecola State Park along the Pacific and ate some sandwiches Donna had made for us. We then headed for Silverton and arrived at Steffens at 8:30. Stan and Ruth Steffen had coffee and sandwiches for us as well as beds to sleep in. Sara and I got to know Stan and Ruth as Mennonite Your Way guests in our home some years ago.

On Wednesday Seth and Hazel stayed at the Steffens to rest. Sara and I went with Stan and Ruth and among other things enjoyed seeing and exploring the Silverton Falls and the Catholic Monastery and Museum. We ate lunch at a nice little country restaurant. For the evening we drove to the coast where Stan and Ruth had rooms reserved for the four of us on second floor at a Best Western facing the Pacific. After dinner we walked on the beach then went to bed listening to the ocean waves.

On Thursday morning it was low tide and we walked out to large rocks that had all kinds of sea life clinging to them. Heading back to Steffens we spent time at Western Mennonite School and talked with the principal. Back at Steffens we ate, packed up, said good-bye and headed for California about 2:15 pm. Driving south on I5 we first drove through nice farmland then through some forests and mountains and in southern Oregon entered the Cascade Range with snow capped mountains. We entered California around 7:00, took pictures of Mt. Shasta and found a campground near Yreka.

On Friday our car gave out. Going south after crossing I80 at Sacramento our engine overheated. We found a Dodge dealer mechanic at Stocton who flushed the radiator, put on two new belts and a new water hose for $162. We kept going south but the engine got hot again. At Modesto we pulled off of I5 and found a garage that was closed but the deli was open. A man came from the deli, checked our engine and said we have a cracked block or head. We could go no further. We got permission there to set up our pop-up trailer at the corner of the garage/deli parking lot. The gentleman who checked our engine offered us his Pinto station wagon to use while getting our car fixed. So I went home with him, Robert Hansen, and got his Pinto. When I came back a man was talking with Seth and Hazel. The man offered his pickup to pull our trailer out to his home and set up under a tree in his yard. We accepted the offer, got his truck and pulled our trailer onto CD Boone's farm, a German Baptist. His wife was visiting her sister in Georgia so it was just CD and his son Joshua at home. They have orange trees in their yard by our trailer.

On Saturday morning Seth and I made some local calls trying to find a garage to help us but found none. Two men, Brian Graybill and Ray Denlinger, working in CD's welding shop near our trailer came to help us. They found a garage in nearby Salida, someone they knew. They towed our car to the garage for us.

On Sunday Sara and I borrowed CD's pickup and went to Mennonite Community Church in Fresno. James Wenger is pastor there. James is a brother to John Wenger from Iowa who was in Greece when I was. Afterward Sara and I drove through Kings Canyon and Sequoia National Parks, both fantastic parks. Leaving Sequoia on the southwest we drove through Three Rivers where Seth was in Civilian Public Service or CPS. But Seth was not along to show us where the CPS camp was. We got back to CD Boones at 10:00, a 400 mile trip.

The five days at Boones waiting for our car we explored local almond and orange groves, visited bookstores in Modesto, played Shanghai, Rummikub and other games, made phone calls and relaxed under the tree where our trailer was.

Wednesday morning we took CD's van, returned the Pinto, drove to Salida and got our car. On the road again we toured Yosemite with many water falls, boulders, canyons and large trees. It was great! We then arrived at Alvin Lapps near Coleville before dark. Alvin is Seth and my nephew. Alvin and his wife Sue were expecting us. Alvin is Wildlife Habitat Manager for State Fish and Wildlife Services in southern California. After a good breakfast Thursday morning he took us up on the mountain range where he works with his four wheel drive vehicle.

We left Alvins Thursday and drove through Reno, Nevada where we got on I80. At Reno while waiting at a traffic light a guy on a motorcycle right beside us waved. Sara rolled down her window and he asked, "Kennet dir Deutsch schvetsa?" (Can you speak German?) Sara said we could and asked him where he was from. He said, "Fleetwood" and we both took off with the traffic. We drove through many salt marshes and seemingly wasteland in Utah but had a nice stop at Salt Lake City, driving past the Temple and Capitol. We needed to have a 1,000 mile check-up on our car but could find no garage to do it. We finally called ahead to a

Dodge dealer in Brigham City and made an appointment. Following that we made our way toward Yellowstone National Park. Afton and Jackson in Wyoming were especially interesting as was driving through Teton National Park. It was almost dark when we arrived at Yellowstone but we got a cabin for the night near Old Faithful Geyser for $39.00. Our car did not take hills very well.

We spent much of Saturday in Yellowstone. We saw Old Faithful erupt, drove by Yellowstone Lake, saw deer, bear and buffalo. Many scenes of the canyon were fantastic. We crawled up the steep mountain roads. We left by the Northwest Exit into Montana toward evening, traveled north to I 90 following the Yellowstone River. Sunday morning we stopped at Terry, Montana, where Seth had spent a year or so in CPS and we saw where the CPS camp was. We expected to attend the Mennonite church at Glendive but no one was there when we arrived at 10:00. I called Pastor Jonas Beachy and was informed that Glendive and Bloomfield congregations were together at a camp setting for the Memorial Day holiday. In our phone conversation I discovered Jonas was a brother to John Beachy of Scottdale, Pa whom I knew and that he lived in Loman, Minnesota when I was there in Bible School in 1951 and in 1953. Because of very strong head wind and poor compression on our small engine we could not go over 45 mph. We got through North Dakota to a campground just east of Fargo ND in Moorhead, Minnesota.

On Monday the headwinds weren't as strong and it felt good to travel 55 mph. We saw Amish in several communities in Wisconsin before arriving at the home of Marvin and Naomi Schwartz in Spencer. We spent the evening and Tuesday morning with Marvins and had an enjoyable time. Naomi is Seth and my niece, the daughter of our sister Lizzie Miller. On Tuesday we left Spencer soon after 8:00, drove south through Chicago and arrived at Sister Lizzie's home in Bremen, Indiana around 5:30. David was mowing and crimping grass. I helped with the milking. David and Linda and Eli and Edith joined us at Lizzies for supper and the evening.

Wednesday we visited Marvin Musser in Nappanee where he works in a shoe store, had lunch at Eli and Edith's then went to Goshen. At Goshen Seth and Hazel visited Hazel's cousin, Sara and I visited Bertha Beachy at Provident Bookstore and had supper with Mose and Ada Beachy. Ada is Sara's sister. In the evening we visited briefly with Lloyd and Mary Schwartz and family at Etna Green. Had ice cream and pie before we left. Mary is Sister Lizzie's daughter. We spent the night at Sister Lizzies.

On Thursday we drove home from Sister Lizzies in Bremen arriving in Buena Vista at 9:00. We traveled over 9,900 or almost 10,000 miles. A wonderful trip.

CHAPTER 19

Kykotsmovi, Grand Canyon, San Diego, Richard Rohr

For his transculture requirement at Eastern Mennonite College Herman did student teaching at a Navajo Middle school in Ganado, Arizona in 1995. It was a good experience for him and evidently kindled his interest and fascination with Native Americans and their reservations because he spent approximately 12 of his next 14 years teaching in Native American Schools in Arizona. He taught one year in a Navajo School and the rest in two Hopi Schools.

Sara and I were very curious what it might be like on an Indian Reservation so in the fall of 1997 decided to find out and planned a trip West. Like usual we visited family, friends and places of interest along the way and that's what this and the final chapter are about. In 1997 Herman was in his second year at Kykotsmovi Mission School on the Hopi Reservation in Arizona. His first year was Voluntary Service and his second year he was hired as a teacher. So on Friday September 19 Sara and I left home in our 91 Camry for a three week trip west. Our first stop was for supper at Mose and Ada Beachys in Goshen, Indiana. Ada is Sara's sister. We then went to my sister Lizzie Miller near Bremen overnight.

On Saturday we drove from Bremen, Indiana to Hutchinson, Kansas, a distance of 860 miles to be with my brother John and his wife Floy. John had recently retired from being a pastor over 30 years at Birch Grove Mennonite Church in Port Allegany, Pa. He and Floy were now serving in Mennonite Voluntary Service in Hutchinson.

180

On Sunday we worshiped with them at Faith Mennonite. We also visited Amish Bishop John Mast who had Dad's funeral sermon in 1975. Brother John and I had some long chats together.

From Hutchinson we drove to Rocky Ford, Colorado to visit John and Floy's daughter Ruth Ann married to John Zimmerman, a pastor, and their son Caleb. Spent the night with them then had a wonderful trip through the Rockies to Bloomfield, NM where we visited Richard and Esther Miller Hochstetler. Esther is my niece. We were with them overnight and on Wednesday morning Esther went with Sara and me to visit Aden Gingerich at Lamp and Light Publishing House. Aden is an old friend of mine from Plain City, Ohio who as an Amish boy graduated from Lancaster Mennonite High School in Pennsylvania. Leaving Bloomfield we stopped at Four Corners and Canyon de Chelly and arrived at Kykotsmovi Mission School around 3:45. Herman was just ready to go to a track meet at Second Mesa with his students so we went with them.

Thursday September 25 was a special day for me. I had hiked to the top of Pikes Peak in the Colorado Rockies and I dreamt that someday I could hike to the bottom of the Grand Canyon. Because Herman could only have one day off from teaching and we had no reservations to stay at Phantom Ranch at the bottom of the Canyon along the Colorado River our only choice was a one-day hike which Herman and I decided to do. Sara, Herman and I left Herman's house at 4:30 and at 6:25 Herman and I started hiking down Bright Angel Trail. There were some signs posted not to attempt a one day hike down and back but we did not heed them. The Canyon walls of Bright Angel Trail of various colors, heights and depths were just beautiful, indescribable really. We arrived at the Colorado River at 11:00. In talking with another hiker he told us Phantom Ranch is really not far upriver. We could go there and go back up Kaibab Trail which we decided to do. We did walk over the bridge to Phantom Lodge and back and started walking up

Kaibab Trail at 11:30. Kaibab was different from Bright Angel but likewise indescribably beautiful. Also very steep and very long and eventually I got very tired. After some time my legs were hurting and near the top I had to stop and rest every five or ten minutes. But I finally made it! At the top we could not find Sara. Herman thought maybe she walked down Bright Angel Trail to meet us. He checked it out and found her waiting for us on the Trail. We arrived back at Herman's house by 8:30. It was a full and fulfilling day for me!

Friday, Saturday and Sunday we took it easy but Herman kept us involved in interesting things. He had us help a friend take sweet corn out of a pit where it roasted, took us to Old Oraibi. Old Oraibi is one of the oldest continuously inhabited settlements in the United States. He found a place for us to sit on a flat house-roof near the finish line of a two mile foot race on top of First Mesa and took us to a community dance on Second Mesa. On Sunday we participated in the Oraibi Mennonite Church then drove to Ganado where Herman had done his student teaching. We also just sat out under the stars.

On Monday Sara and I said good-bye to Herman and drove to San Diego to visit Bill and Marilyn Zuspan. Bill had a life changing experience while studying under Tony Compolo at Eastern College. Later he and Marilyn lived near our home because a daughter lived nearby. They attended Sandy Hill Mennonite Church, Sara and my home church. Bill served as a spiritual mentor for me for about a year but moved to San Diego because another daughter lived there. We had a great time together in San Diego. On Wednesday we drove to Phoenix and stayed with Gene and Neta Buckwalter Kimmel, also Sandy Hill Mennonite Church friends.

From Phoenix we went to The Center for Action and Contemplation begun by Richard Rohr in Albuquerque. I had heard Richard speak at an MCUSA Assembly at I think Purdue University and I was very impressed. When he began his Retreat Center in Albuquerque I thought it would be a worthwhile place to visit so I took this opportunity to do so. We had reservations so we ate with everyone there on Thursday evening, slept in the Guest House and participated in their prayer time on Friday morning. It was a fulfilling experience. Leaving the Retreat Center we drove south to the Bosque Farms with whom we had some connections then had a great drive to Goldie Zook in Weatherford, OK, a Mennonite Your Way home. Goldie gave us a tour of nearby Thomas and the Et Cetra shop where she works.

Our next stop was with Ken and Judy Nelson at Little Rock, AR. At the Nelsons we listened to the "Lobe Song" on tape as it is sung in Amish Churches every Sunday. We went with Ken and Judy to the Lutheran Church where we participated in communion. Ken took the two year course at Shalem that I did and we became friends. It was when they later visited us in our home that we discovered Judy, a little Lutheran girl in Minnesota and I, a little Amish boy in Pennsylvania, said the same prayer as we knelt by our bed before sleeping each evening. I refer to this in chapter 1 and chapter 12.

From Little Rock we had two more stops before returning home. Our first stop was at Joe and Mary Millers at Guthrie, Kentucky. They have a large farm. Joe is Sara's brother. We then went to Aaron and Ida Troyers at Crossville, Tennessee. They have a store and a welding and repair shop. Ida is Sara's sister. While at Crossville we visited the Christian Community near Cooksville where they have no gas engines or electricity in their community. Some of their power comes from horses on a treadmill. Elmo Stoll is founder of the community. From Crossville Sara and I drove to Sparta and had supper with Marvin and Naomi Miller Schwartz. Naomi is a niece of mine. We arrived home Wednesday eve October 8, an interesting, fun and worthwhile trip of 7,000 miles.

CHAPTER 20

Havasu Canyon
and Other Trips West

After having only one day to experience the Grand Canyon Herman wanted us to experience a weekend in a campground in Havasu Canyon down river some miles from the Grand Canyon. This, my final chapter, includes this unique event. The campground is a ten mile hike from the top of the canyon with no roads. The only access is by walking, riding a donkey or horse or a helicopter. Eight miles down the trail is the village of Supai where the helicopter is stationed.

Sara and I left home on Friday, October 1, 1999 for this trip. We spent the weekend in Holmes County, Ohio, which included a 75th birthday surprise party for Sara's sister Mabel at Bethel Church. Monday night we were with my sister Lizzie Miller near Bremen, Indiana. Our next stop was with Titus and Hannah Graber in Richmond, Missouri. Hannah is Sara's niece. Titus told us of his recent trip to India. John and Ruth Ann Lapp Zimmerman at Rocky Ford, again gave us lodging as they had on our 1997 trip. On our way to Rocky Ford we had lunch at the Dutch Restaurant in Hutchinson, Kansas, as we often do on our trips west.

Irene wanted to experience this camping weekend with us so she flew to Albuquerque and we picked her up at the Bosque Farms just south of Albuquerque owned and operated by the DeSmett family. Dennis DeSmett, one of the boys, had been in our home with his friend Dave Klingensmith Jr. from Sandy Hill Mennonite

Church a time or so thus we had some connections. Sara, Irene and I then had a very nice drive to Ganada, Arizona, where Herman was teaching I think Middle school. On Friday while Herman was teaching, Sara, Irene and I spent some time at nearby Hubbell Trading Post, a National Historic Site. It is one of the oldest trading posts in the US.

Friday afternoon at 3:00 we left in two vehicles for Hualapai Hilltop on top of Hualapai Canyon. We stopped at Conrads, Herman's friends in Flagstaff, left our Camry there and we all got into Herman's pickup which was loaded with camping equipment and food. We arrived on top of the canyon at 9:30 and tried to sleep in our sleeping bags. None of us slept much. We ate our breakfast, packed our backpacks with food and camping equipment and started down the Hualapai Canyon Trail at 8:20. The first two miles we had many switchbacks which made it interesting and scenic. The next six miles to the village of Supai was often on the level, not as interesting and a rather long six miles. I can hardly believe Sara did it but she did and seemed to enjoy it. She had a very light backpack. We really looked forward to reaching Supai as we were somewhat tired, dirty and hungry and expected Supai to be an oasis of sorts. Because of my high expectations Supai was disappointing. The individual homes seemed rather dirty including the children, no green grass as expected and we walked a while before finding a store. We got our camping permit then had two more miles to walk. Herman went ahead to get a camping spot for us. It may be of interest that Glen Lapp lived and worked in Supai for a year or so as a registered nurse. Some years later while with MCC in Afghanistan Glen with a medical team of 10 was ambushed and everyone killed in August of 2010.

On our additional two mile hike to the campground in Havasu Canyon Sara and I stopped to rest and relax at the Havasu Falls, two streams running down side by side over the 120 ft falls into a pond. Herman and Irene joined us and we spent an enjoyable two or more hours there. Continuing to the Havasupai Campground where Herman had set up our tent we had a good supper together. Most of the campsites were filled with 100 or more people. Everyone there had walked 10 miles or ridden on a donkey, mule or horse to get there. We all had a good night's sleep.

On Sunday morning after having coffee together Irene and I walked the two miles to the village, attended church there and had lunch at the Cafe. I called Goldie Zook in Oklahoma from a pay phone and made arrangements for Sara and me to stay there Tuesday night. Back at camp we read and talked and walked a mile down the trail to Mooney Falls where we had fun walking under the falls. The Colorado River is six more miles down the trail and we did not go. Back at camp about dark Sara went to the row of toilets about a five or ten minute walk. A half hour or so later she had not returned and it was dark. I walked up to the toilets and she was not there. Sara had especially noted our neighbor's lit lantern as a landmark when she left and when she returned the lantern was not lit anymore and she kept on walking. She walked to the end of the campground and turned around but had no idea where our tent was. The three of us were walking around in the dark looking for her and we did find her. She was not overly stressed because she assumed we would find her.

I did not sleep well Sunday night. We got up at 5:00, broke camp and started up the ten mile trail at 6:30. Because Sara was tired it took us an hour and fifteen minutes to get to Supai, a two mile hike. Herman and Sara stayed there, had breakfast and at 11:00 Sara left by helicopter. She was out in 4 ½ minutes and waited for us. Irene and I got up at 12:30 and Herman about ten minutes later. We drove to Conrads in Flagstaff, got our Camry that was parked there then Irene, Sara and I drove to Gallup, NM and got a Budget Motel for three for $40.00. Herman drove to

Ganada. From Gallup the three of us went to DeSmetts at Bosque Farms, left Irene there, got an oil change for our car, and Sara and I drove to Goldie Zooks at Weatherford OK. Goldie is a Mennonite Your Way place and we had stayed with her in 1997. On Wednesday we drove 800 miles to Guthrie KY, to Joe and Mary Millers. Joe is Sara's brother. We had breakfast with Joe and Mary. Sara and I then enjoyed beautiful fall foliage as we drove 720 miles to Catlett, Virginia and stayed with Freda Miller, Sara's niece. Freda works at Golden Rule Travel Agency. Golden Rule also represents a telephone company and we switched our telephone from MCI to Golden Rule while there. We arrived home Friday afternoon October 15, a trip of 5,400 miles. Sara and I were very grateful to Herman for arranging our unforgettable experience in the Havasupai Campground in the Havasu Canyon.

Herman lived in Arizona approximately 12 years and in 2009 moved to Salida, Colorado where he now lives with his wife Farrah Fine. He teaches math. In 2007 Irene moved to Salida, Colorado and now lives in Buena Vista, Colorado with her husband Marty Ryan. Irene works in a bank. She and Marty are considering moving to North Carolina this fall. Because our children lived in these two states Sara and I made at least nine trips west to visit them. And just for my benefit I am outlining these trips here which you can skip and you won't miss anything.

Our trips to Arizona and Colorado:

September 19-October 8, 1997 (see chapter 19)
October 1-October 15, 1999 (see chapter 20)

AUGUST 11-AUGUST 29, 2003

Slept at David and Linda's then stopped at Mose and Ada Beachys, also met Uncle Dan, Marvin Musser and Arlin and Naomi Hunsberger, were at IHOP in Kansas City, MO and visited

Nedra and Dan Rutherford. Spent several days at the Greek Pax Reunion in Aurora, Nebraska and a day with Shorty and Sophie Jantzi at their home. Visited Joy Lapp and Steve Ruby in Boulder, CO. Had a Mennonite Your Way with Ray and Gail Davis in Colorado Springs. Stayed with Richard and Esther Hochstetler in Bloomfield NM, also Aden Gingerich. Were with Herman at Hotevilla Thursday eve to Monday morning. Met Winona Houser there, took a trip to Monument Valley in Utah and slept at Mexican Hat. Coming home we visited Ken and Judy Nelson in Sedona and Paul and Linda Beiler in Phoenix. Met Oliver Troyer at Dutch Kitchen in Hutchinson. Stayed in motels two nights and our last night at John and Tena's.

OCTOBER 22-NOVEMBER 4, 2007

First stop with sister-in-law widow Mary Miller in Penchem near Guthrie KY. Stopped at Tim and Wilma Beachy's in Harrison AR, Richard and Esther Hochstetler in Hale Center Texas then Irene in Salida. Met Marty. Visited the Amish Community in Monte Vista. Coming home we picked up Mose Beachy at Canon City, came to Hutchinson and stayed with Bill and Thea Klassen. Ate with Ruth Ann Lapp Zimmerman at Mt. Pleasant Iowa at Dutch Family Restaurant and stayed with David and Verna Yoder for the night, Mose Beachy's sister. Left Mose at Goshen, slept at Sister Lizzies in Bremen then to Brother David's in Holmes for a night. Nates put a new roof on their house while we were gone and Smucker Brothers put an awning over our deck.

SEPTEMBER 8-SEPTEMBER 19, 2008

Left Lancaster Monday pm by AMTRAK, changed trains at Pittsburgh and Chicago, arrived at Glenwood Springs CO at 5:00 pm Wednesday evening. The Rockies were fantastic from Denver to Glenwood Springs. Irene met us at Glenwood and

took us to their home in Salida. Sara, Irene and I went to a high
point of Monarch Pass in a gondola. Sara and I took Irene's Toyo-
ta pickup and drove to Hotevilla to visit Herman, a four day trip.
Drove through Durango and Pagosa Springs on our way back to
Salida. Stayed at a hotel in Glenwood Springs with Irene Tuesday
night and got on AMTRAK at 2:00 pm, again a very scenic ride
to Denver. Took a Trailway bus from Galesburg, Illinois to To-
ledo Ohio to catch our train to Pittsburgh which we would have
missed in Chicago. Karen picked us up at Lancaster AMTRAK at
2:30 Friday afternoon.

MAY 23-JUNE 12, 2011

Drove from home to David and Linda's in Bremen. Visited
Lloyd and Mary Schwartz and were told Lloyds are bringing 12
horses to Horse Progress Days in Spring Garden, PA over July 4.
Slept at Christ and Marys at Goshen. Picked up Mose Beachy
and the three of us came to John and Ruth Anns at Mt. Pleasant. Also visited with Joy and Steve at Mt. Pleasant. Drove from
there to Hutchinson where I had a slight accident while turning
in to Dutch Restaurant and lost the passenger side mirror. We are
staying with Paul and Martha Miller. Drove to Colorado Springs
and dropped off Mose to be with his boys Paul and John. Marty,
Irene and Herman met us at Paul's place. Mose treated all of us
at Country Buffet for supper. Sara went with Irene and Marty to
Buena Vista and Herman and I went in our Civic. On Sunday we
drove to LaJara to find the Amish Community, saw where church
was, drove in and met Merv Fisher, grandson of Elam and Flor-
ence Fisher from Buyerstown. On Memorial Day Herman and
Farrah took Irene and me for a raft ride down the Arkansas River
which I thoroughly enjoyed. We also visited the Amish Community in Westcliffe where we met Wilbur Yoder at Yoders Mountain View Furniture Store. Wilbur is the preacher for the eight

Amish families there. He also has a solar business. We stopped by where Joel and Ruth Troyer from Holmes County were building their home near the foot of a mountain eight miles south of West-cliffe. Visited the Bishop's Castle then the Mennonite Thrift Store in Canon City. Coming home, we went to Partridge, Kansas and stayed at Jay and Verna Mae Millers for the night. Had breakfast at Dutch Kitchen then went to Bethel College to be part of the Greek Pax Reunion. Met LaMar and Kathryn Stauffer, Norman Kennel, Loyal and Bertha Klassen, Larry and Anetta Eisenbeis, Elbert and Zola Esau and others I knew. Gerald and Sophie Jantzi joined us later. Got a new mirror put on the Civic for $220.00. After the reunion Sara and I took a 95 mile drive by Hesston College, McPherson, Hillsboro and Taber College. We stayed at Voth Hall at the College yet for Sunday night. Monday we met Mose at Dutch Kitchen and had Dorothy Fisher as our waitress. Arrived at Goshen on Tuesday, met Uncle Dan and Aunt Anna and were to Barbs for supper and overnight. Mose came with us to Holmes County where Mose and Amy Miller are hosting the Abe and Fannie Miller Reunion. 75 or 80 of us were roasting hot dogs outside then it rained and we went into the large shed. On Saturday we visited the graveyard and had a memorial service for Grandpa and Grandma Miller. On Sunday during our service we included a brief memorial for the four Millers no longer with us, Mabel, Ada, Abe and Joe. Sara and I arrived home Sunday eve, a 4,800 mile trip.

SEPTEMBER 24-OCTOBER 3, 2012

Mel Smoker took Sara and me to Lancaster where we board-ed AMTRAK Tuesday at 1:52, as did Sam and Lydia Beiler from Bird in Hand who are on their way to visit their and Seth Fisher's grandchildren in Little Falls, Montana. Irene and Herman picked us up at La Junta and took us to nearby Cheraw where we met Pastor John Stoltzfus. On Thursday noon in Salida I gave a 20 minute Appalachian Trail presentation to forty of Herman's 7th grade boys. On Friday Sara and I bought an extension table and four chairs for Herman and Farrah at Yoder's Furniture in Westcliffe. On Saturday Jack and Judy Fine, Farrah's parents, were with us. On Monday Farrah took Sara and me to Denver where we got the California Zephyr for Chicago. Changed trains there and Nathan picked us up at Lancaster at 1:35 pm.

OCTOBER 16-20, 2014

Josh took Sara and me to the Philly airport. Left Philly at 10:20 am. Thursday arrived in Denver 2:15 our time, 12:15 local. Herman met us and brought us to Salida. On Friday Herman pulled Sara on a bike trailer all over downtown Salida. It was fun. We hiked on the Continental Divide Trail at Marshall Pass. Irene and Marty took Sara and me to Hotchkiss where we were informed there is an Amish Community. However, they are plain Mennonite, not Amish. But it was an enjoyable, scenic drive. Sunday Irene and I attended the Episcopal Church. On Monday Irene took us to the Denver Airport. We arrived at the Philly airport at 7:30 pm and Nathan met us.

JULY 5-11, 2017

Mike took Sara and me to Philly Airport and we left for Denver soon after 9:00 pm. Herman met us and put us up in a Hyatt Hotel. Thursday he took us to Canon City where we boarded a train on the Royal Gorge Route Railroad and traveled seven miles along the gorge and back. We were under the high Royal Gorge bridge. Stopped at an Amish Gift Shop and met a van load of Amish from Holmes County. On Saturday Herman, Irene Sara and I drove to Pagosa Springs where we met John and Michelle Lapp. John is Christ Lapp's Jakes' son, our neighbor. Had a nice visit and a nice drive. On Monday Herman and Farrah took us to the Denver Airport and stopped at Jack and Judy Fines, Farrah's parents on the way. Nate met us at the Philly Airport Tuesday morning soon after 1:00.

Conclusion

At age 87 and now having written my memoirs, what is my conclusion? I ponder why I made certain decisions. The home farm was to be mine but I went to Pax instead of staying on the home farm. Why did I disappoint my parents and my church and go to college? Why marry Sara Ellen Miller? Work at Provident? Take a Marriage Encounter Weekend? I had many choices in my life and I did not always make good choices. I believe God was always with me even when I made bad choices and experienced the consequences. Possibly the most far reaching decision I made in my life was to go into Pax instead of staying on the farm. God blessed that decision. It was life changing and led to a fulfilling life. However I believe God would also have blessed my life had I decided to be an Amish farmer. It just would have been different. I do not believe God made me make my choices. I believe God helped me make my choices when I asked Him to but more than one choice would have been okay.

I have learned through the years to take my beliefs more lightly and walk more humbly. I don't know as much as I used to and even what I think I know is likely not all true. And I'm comfortable with that. An Old Testament scripture that I feel summarizes the message of the Prophets is Micah 6:8, "He has told you, O mortal, what is good; and what does the Lord require of you but to do justice, and to love kindness, and to walk humbly with your God?" This is a very helpful passage for me. And Jesus said that loving God and neighbor is fulfilling the law and the Prophets. Matthew 22:36-40. This is more important than anything else according to Jesus! I try to remember that. Jesus also said we are not to judge others. Presently I try to make Psalm 37:3 my own, "Trust in the Lord and do good." Amen

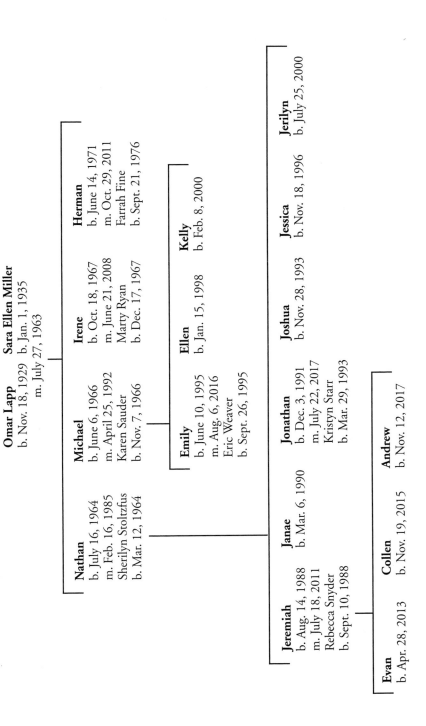

Omar Lapp
b. Nov. 18, 1929

Sara Ellen Miller
b. Jan. 1, 1935
m. July 27, 1963

Nathan
b. July 16, 1964
m. Feb. 16, 1985
Sherilyn Stoltzfus
b. Mar. 12, 1964

Michael
b. June 6, 1966
m. April 25, 1992
Karen Sauder
b. Nov. 7, 1966

Irene
b. Oct. 18, 1967
m. June 21, 2008
Marty Ryan
b. Dec. 17, 1967

Herman
b. June 14, 1971
m. Oct. 29, 2011
Farrah Fine
b. Sept. 21, 1976

Emily
b. June 10, 1995
m. Aug. 6, 2016
Eric Weaver
b. Sept. 26, 1995

Ellen
b. Jan. 15, 1998

Kelly
b. Feb. 8, 2000

Jeremiah
b. Aug. 14, 1988
m. July 18, 2011
Rebecca Snyder
b. Sept. 10, 1988

Janae
b. Mar. 6, 1990

Jonathan
b. Dec. 3, 1991
m. July 22, 2017
Kristyn Starr
b. Mar. 29, 1993

Joshua
b. Nov. 28, 1993

Jessica
b. Nov. 18, 1996

Jerilyn
b. July 25, 2000

Evan
b. Apr. 28, 2013

Collen
b. Nov. 19, 2015

Andrew
b. Nov. 12, 2017

Christian K. Lapp
b. Mar. 21, 1826
m. Feb. 13, 1851
d. Aug. 24, 1878

Annie (Nancy) Stoltzfus
b. Mar. 27, 1831
d. July 1, 1916

David F. Stoltzfus
b. Apr. 26, 1826
d. Apr. 2, 1896

Sarah Mast
b. Nov. 13, 1828
d. May 3, 1892

Samuel Blank
b. Jan. 1, 1831
m. Dec. 27, 1855
d. 1867

Hannah Stoltzfus
b. Mar. 3, 1833

Benjamin Lantz
b. Mar. 8, 1838
d. Sept. 21, 1912

Susan Lapp
b. Mar. 31, 1839
d. Nov. 30, 1905

John H. Lapp
b. Oct. 8, 1854
p.b. Lancaster Co., PA
m. Dec. 26, 1878
d. Jan. 15, 1931
p.d. Gap, PA

Rachel Stoltzfus
b. Feb. 16, 1858
p.b. Lancaster Co., PA
d. Feb. 22, 1934
p.d. Gap, PA

Christian S. Blank
b. Aug. 21, 1861
p.b. Lancaster Co., PA
m. Dec. 18, 1883
d. Mar. 26, 1942
p.d. New Holland, PA

Elizabeth S. Lantz
b. July 13, 1864
p.b. Lancaster Co., PA
d. Sept. 8, 1951
p.d. New Holland, PA

Moses Lapp
b. Jan. 7, 1885
p.b. Gap, PA
m. Nov. 29, 1910
d. Sept. 16, 1975
p.d. Gap, PA

Rachel Blank
b. May 12, 1888
p.b. New Holland, PA
d. Oct. 10, 1977
p.d. Gap, PA

Omar Lapp
b. Nov. 18, 1929,
p.b. Gap, PA
m. July 27, 1963

Sara Miller
b. Jan. 1, 1935,
p.b. Holmes County, OH